ERNEST WILSON

SMOKE
THAT THUNDERS

I0892780

WATERSTONE • LONDON

Waterstone & Co. Limited
49 Hay's Mews
London WIX 7RT

All Rights Reserved.

First published in the U.S.A. in 1927 as *Plant Hunting Vol. 1*

This edition first published by
Waterstone & Co. Limited © 1985.

ISBN 0 947752 25 0

Front cover: 'Entrance to Otira Gorge, New Zealand'
by Marianne North. Crown Copyright ©. Reproduced with
permission of the Controller, Her Majesty's Stationery Office
and the Trustees, Royal Botanic Gardens, Kew.

Back cover: Olearia Insignis T.7034 from
Botanical Magazine vol. 115. Copyright of the Trustees of the
Royal Botanic Gardens, Kew © 1985. Reproduced with
permission.

Cover Design by Carol Brickley at Boldface.

Printed and bound in Great Britain by
Richard Clay (The Chaucer Press) Ltd,
Bungay, Suffolk.

Distributed (except in USA) by
Thames and Hudson Ltd

To
THOSE OF EVERY RACE AND CREED
WHO HAVE LABORED IN DISTANT LANDS TO MAKE
OUR GARDENS BEAUTIFUL THIS VOLUME
IS DEDICATED

PREFACE

From 1899 when I paid my first visit to China until 1922, when I sailed home from Cape Town in South Africa, I wandered about the world in search of plants. This has been a great and privileged experience and one thoroughly enjoyed. My travels have been largely off the beaten tracks but some of them led over ground hallowed by memories of early plant hunters.

In this volume I have attempted to give some account of the lands visited, of their discovery, their vegetation, and, to tell in a general way also of the work done by early plant hunters. All parts of the world have added to the common store of garden material but the countries sketched are among the richest sources of supply. Such a task as here attempted must, of course, be discursive since finality is obviously impossible. I have merely lifted a corner of the curtain so as to allow a peep at the general scene.

Often I am asked which of the countries I have visited I like the best but have found no ready answer. Every land is rich in interest with abundance to see, study and enjoy. Wherever I have travelled I have found handsome trees and beautiful flowers, likewise, kindly folk among all sorts and conditions of people. I look back with pleasure and gratitude to each and every country visited. This is not the place but it would be easy to fill a book with the names of pleasant, helpful people I have met.

In this age it is a great pity that botany does not figure as an essential item in the education of everyone. A little knowledge of plants would add enormously to the pleasure and interest derived from visits near and far – a walk near home, a motor ride through neighboring country or a trip to a foreign land. To be able to recognize and interpret the things around vastly increases the joy of living. It is a truism that the more one knows about plants the more interesting they become and the greater the enjoyment derived from their association. Plants with their beauty of form, of leaf and of flower appeal to all and the history of how, when and from whence they came should add to the pleasure we derive from their presence. Nature is a generous mother and with flower and leaf has decked the world in loveliness. Love of the beautiful in organic or inorganic life is the most elevating influence permeating the human family. There are no happier folk than plant-lovers and none more generous than those who garden. There is a delightful free-masonry among them, they mingle on a common plane, share freely their knowledge and with advice help one another over

PREFACE

the stepping stones that lead to success. It is truthfully
said that a congenial companion doubles the pleasures
and halves the discomforts of travel and so it is with the
brotherhood who love plants.

E. H. W.

Arnold Arboretum,
Harvard University,
May 15, 1927.

CONTENTS

PART I

AFRICA, SOUTH AND CENTRAL

PART I.

Africa, South and Central

SUNLIT LANDS WHENCE CAME GLADIO-
LUS AND A THOUSAND OTHER FAMILIAR
PLANTS THAT GLADDEN LIVES WITH
THEIR BEAUTY

SOUTH AFRICA

CHAPTER I.

First Visitors and What They Found There

IGHTED in 1487 by Bartholomew Diaz on his return voyage to Portugal, after he had been driven by storms as far east as Algoa Bay, and circumnavigated by Vasco da Gama ten years later, the discovery of the Cape of Good Hope marked an epoch in the world's history. A new all sea-route to India was found, and the wealth of the Indies, barred by the presence of the Crescent in Constantinople and the region bordering the eastern part of the Mediterranean Sea, was accessible to the Christian sea-roving nations of western Europe, of which at the time Portugal was the leading. Diaz from his bitter experience named this southern headland of Africa the Cape of Storms, but his king, from the promise of good things to come, gave it a more cheering name—Bonae Spei— the Cape of Good Hope. That grand old Elizabethan sea-dog, Sir Francis Drake, described it in 1580 as "a most stately thing, the fairest cape we

3

saw in the whole circumference of the earth." And out of numberless points of land on the earth's surface it has appropriated the generic name of "The Cape."

In 1503, a Portuguese, Antonio de Saldanha, put into what is now Table Bay. He was the first European to land on Cape soil and found it to be a very favorable watering place for ships. Later it became famous as such and in old books is referred to as Saldanha Bay and Bonae Spei. On their voyages to and from India the Portuguese occasionally put into Table Bay, but to them the Cape was merely a landmark—much dreaded for the storms that raged round it—to be sighted and gladly passed by. On one occasion (in 1510) at least they fell foul of the inhabitants and the returning first Viceroy of the Portuguese Indies, Francisco de Almeida, and sixty-five of his followers were killed in an attack on a native village. If the Portuguese ever investigated the natural resources of the Cape, which is unlikely, history has preserved no mention of it.

The power of Portugal began definitely to wane about 1580, and then commenced the struggle between the Dutch and English for mastery of the seas. In 1591 the first English ships, three in number under Admiral Raymond, put into Table Bay,

owing to sickness among the crews, and remained
there a month. These were followed in 1598 by
two Dutch ships, the "Lion" and the "Lioness,"
commanded by Cornelis Houtman. Queen Elizabeth,
on December 31, 1600, granted a Royal Charter
to the English East India Company. The Dutch
formed a similar company in March, 1602; the
French in 1604, and the Danes in 1612. My readers may think mention of these old trading compa-
nies of little moment in this connection, but it cannot be too emphatically stated that it is to them
above all other agencies that we owe many of our
most treasured garden possessions from the Cape and
from the Orient, and as we proceed this debt will become more apparent. Those who read thoughtfully
will realize that out of the scramble for the wealth of
the Indies, our gardens enjoy lasting benefits today.

Up to about the middle of the Seventeenth Century Table Bay remained neutral ground for ships of
all nations to water and re-provision, and it became
an established practice for the crews of outward
bound ships to leave letters beneath stones for returning vessels to collect and carry home. But a change
was soon to come and old-time courtesy was replaced
by jealousies and hatred. In 1648, the "Haarlem,"
a ship belonging to the Dutch East India Company,

was wrecked in Table Bay. The crew landed and encamped where Capetown now stands. They sowed seeds, grew vegetables, procured game and fish, and trafficked peaceably with the Hottentot natives for cattle and sheep. For five months these men lived in comfort and plenty until other Dutch vessels arrived and carried them home. On their arrival in the Netherlands two of their number urged upon the Company the desirability of forming a settlement at the Cape. After due consideration the directors of the Company decided to act on the suggestion, and two ships and a small tender were despatched under the command of Jan van Riebeck, in 1652, with orders to build and garrison a fort on the shores of Table Bay. And so it came about that 165 years after Diaz first sighted the Cape of Good Hope, Europeans began permanently to settle in South Africa. The fort was built according to an approved plan large enough to hold from seventy to eighty persons and sufficient ground was appropriated for the purpose of gardening and pasturage. A practical people, the Dutch included one or more gardeners in the original bands of settlers, who numbered about a hundred souls. The station was intended to serve the Dutch trade with the Orient by the victualling of their ships and was, if possible, to be made self-supporting and not to be a drain on the Company's resources.

At this period the Dutch were nearly if not quite the first nation in Europe. In 1655 they drove the Portuguese from Ceylon and made themselves masters of the southern seas. As a halting place for their ships plying to and from the rich possessions in the East Indies, the Cape became of increasing importance to the Dutch. In 1679, a settlement was established some thirty miles inland by Simon van der Stel and named Stellenbosch, and there today flourish magnificent avenues of European Oak (*Quercus robur*), said to have been planted soon after the settlement was founded. The story of the struggle for the possession of the Cape, a struggle vitally connected with that for the admiralty of the seas, fascinating though it be, does not further concern us.

With the settling of the Dutch at the Cape began the introduction of plants into Europe and the first researches into the botany of the region. Our earliest knowledge of Cape plants we owe to Justus Heurnius, whose drawings and descriptions are reproduced by Stapel on pages 333-336 of his edition of "Theophrastus," published in Amsterdam in 1644. Heurnius was Professor of Medicine at Batavia and called at the Cape on his voyage out. He must have been a botanist of no mean order for his figures are very good indeed. *Stapelia variegata, Haemanthus coccineus, Cotyledon orbiculata, Kniphofia aloides* and two species of Oxalis are easily recognized. Linnaeus based the genus Stapelia—a group of characteristic South African plants with short, succulent, tufted stems and curiously mottled star-shaped foetid flowers—on Stapel's figure but it would have been more just had he named it for its discoverer, Justus Heurnius. The first collection of herbarium material of Cape plants was made in 1672 by Paul Herman on his way out to Ceylon to take up his post of chief medical officer to the Dutch East India Company.

By whom the first living plants from the Cape were introduced into Europe is not known but it must have taken place soon after van Riebeck founded the fort if not before. Possibly some of the crew of the wrecked ship "Haarlem" took plants to Holland. At any rate, Jacob Breyne in his "Centuria" published in 1678, tells us that H. de Beveringk had growing in his garden in Holland the plants we now know as *Oxalis purpurea, Mesembryanthemum pugioniforme,* and *Ornithogalum thyrsoides* the poisonous Chinkerichee of the Cape Dutch. Breyne, in the book just mentioned, deals with a

fascicle of rare plants collected at the Cape by
Wilhelm Rhyne in 1673, and received from India
in 1677. A number of these are figured by Breyne,
and very accurate and beautiful are his illustrations
—the first extant—of the lovely scarlet flowered
Erica cerinthoides, the remarkable *Brunia nodiflora,*
the interesting Cape Almond (*Brabejum stel-
latum*), and the now well-known Lion's Tail
(*Leonotis Leonurus*). Quaint old James Petiver
of London in his "Gazophylacii Naturae," II. 9, 10,
tt. 81-90, dated 1709, figures "one hundred elegant
plants growing about the Cape of Good Hope." On
plate 84 are pictures of eight kinds of Pelargonium.
On other plates one recognizes such well-known
plants as the Belladonna Lily (*Amaryllis Belladonna*), *Haemanthus coccineus,* various Aloes,
Mesembryanthemums, Gasterias, Haworthias, and
Stapelias. The bulbous, tuberous and succulent
plants were most easily transported and quite a number of these were in cultivation in Holland and England by the middle of the Eighteenth Century. The
first Cape Heaths (*Erica concinna* and *E. marifolia*)
were not introduced until 1773, so evidently the raising of plants from seeds was found a more difficult
undertaking.

The odd appearance of so many plants and the

beauty of their blossoms excited interest and curiosity among flower-lovers and an eager demand for them grew up. They were designated "Cape Plants," a generic name still in vogue, although a majority of the plants are less known today than they were a century ago. Nevertheless, even today Cape plants are an important unit and some rank among the indispensables. Our Nerines, Freesias, Gladiolus, Clivias, Streptocarpus, Zonale and Regal Pelargoniums are all derived from plants native of the Cape of Good Hope. Our debt to the southern tip of Africa is very considerable, yet it is comparatively light to what it ought to be. The Cape teems with lovely plants suitable for California and the warmer States. The garden spirit has lagged so long in this country that hundreds of plants erstwhile available have disappeared and must be re-sought to the utmost ends of the earth. The story of Cape plants in cultivation is similar to that of Australian plants, though happily, thanks to their bulbous character, a somewhat greater number have survived the neglect of well-nigh a century.

The Cape flora is astounding in both quantity and variety. No accurate figures of the number of species indigenous there are available for the simple reason that its actual wealth has not yet been fully plumbed.

Botanists from Linnaeus in 1753, down to the present day have devoted much time to the naming of Cape plants, but the end is not yet. Many so-called "Floras" of the region have been published, but a complete Flora of the Cape of Good Hope is still a desideratum. Quite recently a botanical survey of South Africa has been inaugurated but the task is colossal and the workers few. This lack of anything like exact knowledge of the number of species of plants indigenous in South Africa is not the fault of botanists. It is the extraordinary richness of the flora that so far has baffled the united efforts of those who have grappled with the problem of its specific classification. The seemingly infinite wealth of plant species may drive the taxonomic botanist to despair but it delights the heart of the garden-lover. So while the botanist figuratively groans beneath the burden, we can skip joyously from one new floral treasure to another—the gardens of America need never lack blossoms of beauty in endless form and variety. The world holds floral treasures beyond the dreams of avarice but it is for us to seek them out and learn how to use them wisely and well.

CHAPTER II.

Joy of Meeting Old Friends

T IS a singularly pleasant emotion that one feels on seeing growing wild for the first time plants which have been familiar friends from earliest memories. This happens very often in travelling through South Africa.

I recall vividly the thrill of delight felt when my eyes first lit on a wild clump of the blue *Agapanthus umbellatus*. It was in Natal and through the window of a railway carriage soon after dawn; how I longed to get out and fondle this old favorite! Similar feelings welled up when first I saw Nerines, Lachenalias, Ixias, *Gladiolus primulinus*, *Kniphofia aloides*, *Asparagus plumosus*, *Watsonia rosea* and other plants. Indeed, my journey through South Africa was a succession of delightful thrills.

The Kniphofias are attractive plants with their yellow, orange and scarlet flowers terminating long stems. Familiarly known as Red-hot Pokers, these plants vary in the height of their flower-stems from less than 1 foot to over 6 feet. Some of the smaller species are singularly beautiful, suggesting a yellow and orange-colored Grape-hyacinth. The favorite *Crinum capense* and *C. Moorei* are South African plants, as also are the Clivias. A wayside weed in many places is *Lobelia coronopifolia* with dark to light blue and white flowers and so, too, is the many-colored *Nemesia strumosa,* from which have been raised within the last few years a pleasing race of annuals. Everlastings in scores of varieties abound but none is more lovely than *Helipterum eximium,* its 6-inch broad corymbs of ruby-red flowers, terminating 3 to 4 feet tall stems which are clothed with broad, woolly leaves.

The scarlet Barbeton Daisy (*Gerbera Jamesonii*) crossed with *G. aurantiaca* and *G. viridifolia* has given rise to a race with florets of many pleasing colors. These Gerberas are now beginning to share a place in gardens with their relatives and fellow-countrymen Gazania and Arctotis. Another modern group of greenhouse flowers we owe to South Africa is Streptocarpus, the Cape Primrose. The race of today—and wonderful it is—is the result of crossing several species and the recrossing, selecting and interbreeding of their progeny. The work was commenced at Kew about 1886 by W. Watson, who pollinated flowers of *Streptocarpus Rexii* from the one-leafed, red-flowered *S. Dunnii.* The resultant hybrid was named *S. kewensis*. He next pollinated flowers of *S. parviflora* from those of *S. Dunnii* and produced a second hybrid which was named *S. Watsonii*. Thus was the foundation laid and to the late Curator of Kew Gardens belongs the credit.

Watsonia is another genus of herbs beautiful in themselves and to the hybridist pregnant with possibilities. In Australia my friend, the late Mr. J. Cronin, Director of the Melbourne Botanic Garden, by intercrossing raised a wonderful race of Watsonias with stems of from 5 to 6 feet tall bearing flowers of every hue. Tritonias are also from South Africa and our gardens today enjoy a beautiful race of these plants as the result of the hybridists' skill and patience in breeding from *Tritonia aurea, T. Pottsii, T. crocata,* and their progeny.

The familiar Calla or Arum Lily (*Zantedeschia aethiopica*) is common in swampy places and alongside rivers from the Cape Province northward to Central Africa and so, too, is a pretty blue-flowered Water-lily (*Nymphaea stellata*), likewise the well-known *Cyperus utilis* and the Cape Pond Weed (*Aponogeton distachyum*). Under a variety of conditions the Lion's Tail (*Leonotis Leonurus*) flourishes; but more particular are the Bird-of-Paradise or Parrot-flowers (*Strelitzia regina, S. augusta,* and

S. parvifolia), relatives of the Banana but with crest-like, brilliant inflorescences rich in honey and much visited by birds.

Among the riches of the Cape flora it is difficult to judiciously pick and choose, but I think this miscellany may end in mention of a group, more familiar the world over perhaps than any plant yet referred to, namely, the common Geranium and Pelargonium of gardens. The parents of the Scarlet Geranium, the Ivy-leaf Geranium and the Regal Pelargonium are Cape plants; and so, too, are the Scented-leaf Geraniums. It is permissible to admire the latter to-day but their gay-flowered relatives are somewhat taboo. Because we have abused these cheery, good-natured plants, made them gross and coarse, over-planted them, and set them in ill-suited places, fashion decrees that for the nonce they be frowned upon. But fashion is a fickle tyrant and it is only a matter of time when she will again smile on old friends. Rightly used the Geranium in its varied forms is one of the most serviceable plants known to gardens, and fie on those who blame the plant for their own misuse of it.

The wild parents of these races of useful plants were among the early introductions from the Cape into Holland, whence they soon were carried to England. The first to arrive appears to have been *Pelargonium cucullatum* in 1690. Paul Herman collected specimens at the Cape in 1672, and figures it on page 275 of his "Horti Academici Lugduno-Bativi Catalogus," issued in 1687, as "Geranium africanum arborescens foliis cucullatis, etc." From this and *P. angulosum* the race of Regal or Show Pelargoniums is considered to have sprung. Of this *P. angulosum*, Martyn in his "Plantae Rariores," published in 1728, gives a good colored figure opposite page 28 under the name of "Geranium africanum arborescens folio anguloso, etc." The plant seems to have reached England a few years previously.

The Ivy-leaf Pelargoniums are derived from *P. peltatum*, which is to be found from a little east of Cape Town eastward to Natal. It is well figured by Caspar Commelin in his "Praeludius Botanicum Plantarum," page 52, fig. 2, published in 1703, as "Geranium africanum foliis asari, etc.," and he says that seeds were received in the year 1700.

The Zonale or Scarlet Geraniums are descended from *P. zonale* and *P. inquinans*, which grow wild around Port Elizabeth, the Algoa Bay of the Portuguese, and elsewhere in the more eastern parts of the Cape. A good illustration of the first-named is given by Caspar Commelin on page 52, fig. 1, of the work

above referred to under the name of "Geranium africanum arborescens Alchemillae hirsuto folio floribus
rubicundis." Commelin states that the seeds had been
received in 1700, from Governor Wilhelm Adrian
van der Stel.   The other species (*P. inquinans*) was
growing in English gardens about 1718, and Martyn, under the name of "Geranium africanum arborescens Malvae folio lucido, etc.," gives an excellent
colored figure of it opposite page 3, in the book
already mentioned.   Maybe these facts and references
to the first known figures may interest the readers
who have a penchant for history.   Be this as it may,
many will envy one so fortunate as to see these famous plants in their native haunts.

CHAPTER III.

The Land as It Is

EFORE proceeding further with the story of the floral treasures of South Africa it is necessary for our proper understanding of the subject to describe as briefly as possible the more outstanding physiographical features of the country. The Cape of Good Hope is now a province of the Union of South Africa. It extends across the southern end of the African continent and has a total area of 276,966 square miles, being slightly larger than the state of Texas. The most southern point is Cape Agulhas in latitude 34°. 50′ south, and the northern boundary about latitude 25°. 40′ south, just beyond the town of Mafeking.

Its physical structure is peculiar and exercises a strong influence on both the climate and the flora. There are four distinct zones, three of which are elevated plateaux. Each is separated by steep escarpments which rise a considerable height above them. The first of these, the coastal plateau or belt, is of very irregular width, varying from about two to thirty miles, is very broken in character, and has an elevation of from sea-level to about 600 feet; in many places the coast-line is bold and the base of the mountains is washed by the sea. No part of the world's surface supports a richer flora than this coastal belt—here luxuriate the wonderful Proteas and their numerous relatives, also the lovely Cape Heaths in hundreds of species. On its western flank are splendid rain-forests forming a belt about 100 miles long and ten miles in width, the only large area of forest in the Cape Province.

North of the coastal region the ground rises more or less abruptly to the Little Karroo, a narrow plateau from fifteen to twenty miles wide with an elevation of from 1500 to 2000 feet. The climate here is much drier and there are no forests, yet the flora is varied and rich. Many shrubs grow there with Aloes, succulent Euphorbias, and miscellaneous tuberous and bulbous plants aplenty; in certain parts Mesembryanthemum dominates extensive areas.

The next plateau is known as the Great or Central Karroo and has an elevation of from 2000 to 3000 feet and extends east and west for some 350 miles. It is a country of shallow soils and rock-strewn surfaces with a low rainfall, and for practical purposes is desert. It is devoid of trees except along the river courses where water flows intermittently. What vegetation there is is largely composed of succulents and small shrubs specially adapted to dry conditions.

Still further inland is the fourth zone, the Northern Karroo, the most extensive of all with an elevation of from 4000 to 6000 feet in the eastern portion. This region enjoys a moderate rainfall and affords excellent grazing and pasturage for all kinds of stock. There are no forests, but low thorny Acacia trees occur scattered through the grasslands together with shrubs in variety and numerous kinds of bulbous plants.

The mountain ranges of the Cape Province are steeply eroded and difficult to cross although the peaks are not high. The highest is under 8000 feet and a majority are under 6000 feet. Table Mountain is 3582 feet with almost sheer precipices guarding its flat summit. The geological record of South Africa is obscure. Owing to the want of fossils in the rocks older than the Devonian there is no means of determining the age of the Palaeozoic system and a local nomenclature has of necessity been invoked. Sandstones and shales of uncertain age and known as the Table Mountain series are a prominent feature throughout much of the Cape. The Karroo is a vast shallow basin filled with sedimentary deposits which are generally regarded as of fresh-water and glacial origin. Marine deposits are confined to the coastal regions and are of minor importance. Granites, characteristic of so much of Africa, only crop out here and there, as at Cape Town for example, and limestone rocks are rare.

The whole of the Cape Province is largely high-level country and its surface configuration has been chiefly determined by the erosive forces exercised by sun, wind and rain. None of the rivers are navigable for any distance and in many water is found only at certain times of the year. A majority of the rivers are steeply graded and the mouths of all are obstructed by sand-bars. All are liable to sudden freshets which sweep down with tremendous force bringing with them great quantities of debris and speedily rendering the fords impassable. Sun and storm have, in truth, laid a heavy hand on the unforested lands of South Africa and the landscape everywhere tells the story plainly. Yet, although erosion has played such an enormous part, the strong ocean currents sweeping the unbroken line of coast have prevented the retention of great sedimentary deposits which in most parts of the world have gone to form fertile plains and deltas at the river mouths.

South Africa is a land of sunshine but the climate generally is cooler than that usually found in similar latitudes in the northern Hemisphere. This is due mainly to the vast ocean to the south of the sub-continent. At Cape Town the maximum is 80°F. and the minimum about 40°F. giving a mean average of 63°F. In the interior the climate is naturally less equable than near the coast. At Cape Town in the west the rainfall is a winter one and averages about forty inches. In the east the rainfall is a summer one and at Port Elizabeth averages about twenty-five inches. On parts of the Karroo it is as little as five inches or even less but on the northern plains it averages from five to twenty inches. Hailstorms are frequent during the winter months but snow, save on the higher mountains, is of rare occurrence. Temperature, winds and the regularity or otherwise of the precipitation of moisture throughout the year, more so than the actual amount of rainfall per year or the chemical nature of the soil, determines the character and richness of a country's flora.

CHAPTER IV.

Floristic Features

APE TOWN is the usual landing place of visitors to South Africa and there is no better place to commence our enquiry into the floral resources of the country. The city is charmingly situated along the shore of Table Bay with Table Mountain rising behind the town in a sheer precipice cutting the skyline with a jagged horizontal front two miles in length. The Cape promontory with its bold head-lands stretches some forty miles south to Cape Point. A narrow sandy neck separates Table and False Bays and joins the promontory to the mainland.

Around Cape Town the Stone or Table Pine (*Pinus pinea*) of Italy and the Cluster Pine (*Pinus pinaster*) of southwestern Europe have been planted in quantity and form magnificent avenues and groves. Nearby are fine plantations of the Monterey or Insignis Pine (*Pinus radiata*) of California. Many other trees, notably the common Oak of Europe (*Quercus robur*) and various Eucalypts, have been extensively planted and it is astonishing how luxuriantly all these exotic trees flourish. The isthmus of shifting sands dividing the bays has been made available for residential purposes by the planting of Maram Grass (*Ammophila arundinacea*) and *Acacia saligna,* a west Australian Wattle. The wild flora of the Cape promontory is remarkable for its wealth and diversity. Proteas and Heaths, succulents and bulbous plants, shrubs and herbs in a riot of species flourish. The unique Silver Tree (*Leucadendron argenteum*) and several other plants are known to grow wild nowhere else. On dripping rock walls high up on Table Mountain flourishes *Disa uniflora,* its flower 5 inches across with bright scarlet sepals and pink labellum, perhaps the most spectacularly beautiful terrestrial Orchid in the world. And there, too, grows the lovely *Anemone capensis* with finely divided leaves and white, suffused with pink, blossoms each 3 inches across and the fine Everlasting *Helichrysum vestitum* whose white heads imported into this country and Europe are much used by florists, to whom they are known as "Capes." The sandy flats have a flora peculiarly their own and where the soil is acid Heaths in endless variety crowd the land. What native trees there are are relegated to the ravines and slopes where they find protection from the winds.

Forests are an infrequent feature of the landscape

throughout the Cape of Good Hope. They are relegated to sheltered nooks and gullies and to the
margins of streams. The coming of the European
with his agricultural schemes has brought about a
great change everywhere throughout the Cape. The
forests have suffered heavily, although never in modern geological times did forests flourish over the face
of South Africa as they do in the temperate regions of
the northern Hemisphere. On the coastal ranges
from near Mossel Bay eastward for a hundred miles
there is a belt some ten miles deep of magnificent rain-
forest. The pretty little village of Knysna is situated
within the extreme edge of this forest and is a con-
venient place from which to investigate it.

Formerly the dominant trees of these forests were
Podocarpus latifolia and *P. falcata* but broad-leaf
trees have long since gained the ascendancy. Where
the woodman's axe has been withheld or lightly used
the Podocarps still tower above the invading hords
of miscellaneous broad-leaf trees, veritable knights of
the forests. A noble tree in particular is *Podocarpus
falcata* with its shapely rounded crown topping a
hundred feet tall, cylindric bole clad with purple-
brown flaking bark. Its relative, *P. latifolia*, is a
somewhat smaller and less striking tree with light
gray fibrous bark but its wood is superior. The

broad-leaf trees of these forests furnish valuable timber but with few exceptions are unknown to the
North. Several are handsome in blossom and among
these mention may be made of the Cape Chestnut
(*Calodendron capense*) with lustrous foliage and
erect masses of large pinkish blossoms. This tree is
much planted for ornamental purposes in Australia
and is also known in Californian gardens. Another
fine tree of moderate size is *Cunonia capensis* with
opposite trifoliolate glossy green leaves and tall
erect paniculate spikes of pure white blossoms.
Reminiscent of the Robinias of this country is
Virgilia capensis with pinnate leaves and pendent
racemes of rose-pink, pea-like flowers. After fires
this is the first tree to spring up and in consequence it
often forms pure colonies but dies out when over-
shadowed by other trees. An ugly tree yet spectacu-
lar when in flower is *Erythrina caffra* common in
open country, but the most pleasing of these Coral
Trees is the dwarf *E. Humeana* with erect racemes of
crimson flowers. On the drier plateaux Acacias in
variety are characteristic trees, either forming thin
woods or merely dotting the countryside. They are
mostly low trees with spreading crowns, fragrant
yellow flower-clusters and all are armed with forbidding thorns. Among the most common are *Acacia*

giraffae, A. karroo, A. Benthamii, A. detinens, A. caffra and *A. spirocarpoides*, on which common names with pointed reference to their thorny character have been bestowed by the native blacks and the Dutch. In warm, dry lands these may be recommended for fencing instead of that modern abomination, barbed wire. Other common trees are the Maroola (*Sclerocarya caffra*), whose branches are beloved of the elephant, and the Wilde Pruimen (*Pappea capensis*), both with plum-like edible fruits. At Bulawayo, near the site of Lo Bengula's kraal, there grows a famous specimen of the Pappea. It is a low tree but has a wide-spreading umbrageous crown and beneath its shade the mighty old Matabele chief was wont to sit and administer rough justice. Hundreds of his people walked from this tree to their death on Thabas Induna, a hill plainly visible some fifteen miles distant to the east.

The genus Rhus is represented by a host of species in South Africa and among other northern genera indigenous there are Ilex, Buxus, Salix, and Celtis, but the species are few. The Taxads of the North are represented by Podocarpus but our genera of Conifers are unknown in South Africa save as planted trees. In rocky places grow several species of Widdringtonia, close relatives of the Australian

Callitris and in habit and general appearance suggestive of our Cupressus. The native Cycads are the curious Stangeria and the mighty Encephalartos, of which *E. caffra,* whose pith is made into a sort of bread by the Kaffirs, is one of the most common. A Tree-fern (*Cyathea Dregei*) is not uncommon in many places, and on Table Mountain and elsewhere grow *Gleichenia polypodioides* and *Todea africana* with its harsh fronds. There are other Ferns and the familiar Bracken is common, but nowhere in the Cape Province are Ferns a feature of the vegetation.

Shrubs in great variety grow on the edge of the forests and the more open country and bright-colored blossoms are the rule. As a large, much-branched bush the well-known *Sparmannia africana* is common round George and also in other districts; there, too, grows *Ochna multiflora,* a most pleasing shrub with small lustrous leaves and yellow flowers which are followed by jet black fruits seated on a thickened scarlet dais. Another old favorite, *Plumbago capensis,* with azure-blue flowers is widespread. I collected it on cliffs near Grahamstown where it is a conspicuous feature.

CHAPTER V.

Honeypots and Silver Tree

S A matter of fact, apart from the very cold regions of the globe, every country can boast of a general miscellany of trees, shrubs and herbs noteworthy for the beauty of their flowers. The Cape we have already shown is no exception and in addition possesses four well-marked types each of sufficient merit to make the country remarkable. These four types—succulent plants, bulbous plants, Proteas and Heaths—dominate the floral features of the Cape of Good Hope. Heaths, bulbous and succulent plants are found in other parts of the world though in less variety but the glorious Proteas are peculiarly South African. Brilliant inflorescences are characteristic of the Cape flora and in this respect the only region in the world with which fair comparisons can be made is Western Australia. In both lands Proteaceae, a family of endless variety of forms, is a striking floristic feature. What the genus Banksia is to Western Australia, Protea is to South Africa; yet this genus is even less known in American gardens than is Banksia. Proteas are common in the immediate vicinity of

Cape Town as well as throughout the whole of the coastal plateau; a few species are found in the more elevated and drier regions to the north. Some, like *Protea grandiflora*, are trees of moderate size, others, like *P. amplexicaulis* and *P. cordata*, almost hug the ground but the vast majority are bushes from 6 to 10 feet tall with erect stems and huge, terminal, handsome heads of flowers. Such heads consist of very many elongated, relatively simple flowers having no petals but with colored calyx and bracts enclosed and nestling within seried rows of tall colored scaly, more or less erect, floral bracts—nests of colored, fluffy down guarded by projecting stamens and pistils suggesting the quills of a fledgling Bird-of-Paradise. The first species to be figured in European literature was *Protea neriifolia* by Clusius in his "Exoticarum" (p. 38, fig. 15) published in 1605, as "Cardui generis elegantissimi, etc." The specimen is said to have come from Madagascar but much more probably it came from the shores of Algoa Bay or those of Table Bay. This species is widespread and its large flower-heads with velvety black apical tufts of hairs bearding the upright involucral scales are strikingly handsome. Nowadays about 100 species are known and all are worth a place in the best Californian gardens, yet Bailey's "Cyclopedia" mentions three only (*P. cynaroides, P. mellifera* and *P. nana*) as in cultivation in this country. Overflowing with honey are the pink and white heads of *P. mellifera,* known to the Boers as "honeypots." The honey is collected and made into a kind of sugar, the blossoming season being a great occasion for picnics. Striking are the inflorescence of *P. speciosa* with tufts of black hairs on the tips of the inner involucral bracts; but none are finer than the glossy-leafed *P. cynaroides* common and widespread from Cape Town to Grahamstown in the east. The involucral bracts of this species vary from nearly white to silvery rose; the heads are from 10 to 12 inches across and the plants from 1 to 10 feet tall. It favors rocky places and to come suddenly upon this plant in blossom, to look down into its wondrous beauty as it nestles amid rocks, is a delight never to be forgotten. It has been my good fortune to see either under cultivation or under their natural conditions nearly all the known flowers of exceptional merit. I have a generous meed of praise for each and every one but, in my judgment, the handsomest inflorescence in the world is that of *Protea cynaroides* seen on its native heath.

Prominent among the renowned trees of the world is the Silver Tree (*Leucadendron argenteum*), the

Witte-boom of the Dutch, which is common on the slopes of the Lion's Head, around Kirstenbosch and elsewhere on granites in the immediate vicinity, but very rare on Table Mountain itself, and quite unknown as a wild tree anywhere else in the world. It is an extraordinary tree which at once arrests attention by its strange appearance. I would not call it beautiful, though it fascinates. About 75 feet is its maximum height, with a crown of proportionate size; the bark is smooth and nearly white becoming roughened and dark in old age; the sessile lance-shaped 6-inch long leaves are densely crowded, clothed with long soft hairs and are silvery gray like the bark. The trees are either male or female and the flowers are not specially attractive, but the fruit is wonderfully interesting. It may be likened to a short, broad, egg-shaped Spruce-cone but it is erect. It has similarly stiff scales, at the base of which nestles a hard, somewhat compressed nut, which is tipped by the style with its thickened club-shaped stigma. These scales are the altered bracts and the nut the fruit proper. Each nut is enclosed within a thin membranous sheath, the persistent calyx, which has four, narrow, densely hairy lobes. When this composite fruit is ripe and the weather dry the "cone-scales" open and in doing so exert pressure on the base of the nut forcing it upward and outward; the calyx-lobes with their tufts of hairs spread quadrilaterally and a perfect parachute is formed. As the wind makes itself felt beneath this parachute the nuts are lifted out, the membranous sheath splits and the nut, now suspended by aid of the persistent style and its thickened stigma, is wafted gently away. The mechanism is marvellous yet the weight of the seed is such that save in strong winds the lateral distance it is carried is slight, indeed it deviates very little from the perpendicular.

Specimens of the Silver Tree were first collected in 1672 by Paul Herman who called it the Atlas Tree. A leafy branch and a naked nut are figured by Plukenet in his "Opera" [I. t. 200 (1691)] under the name of "Leucadendros Africana." A larger figure showing a branch, fruit-cone, nut and parachute is given by Jan Commelin in his "Horti Medici" [pt. 2, 51, t. 26 (1701)] as "Argyrodendros africana, the Witte Boom." Linnaeus called it a Protea and Robert Brown in 1810 gave it the name it has since been known by. The Silver Tree is the despair of the gardener. It is often raised from seed and frequently grows quite freely for a few or several years, and then suddenly dies! It may be added for the consolation of the gardener that even in a wild state at the Cape this tree behaves in the same capricious manner.

More than seventy other species of Leucadendron are recognized, nearly all of them shrubs. One of the most common throughout the coast region is *L. adscendens,* often a dominant feature of the flats and conspicuous by the yellow color of its topmost leaves which are easily mistaken for flowers at a short distance. In the related genus Mimetes the flower heads are small and axillary, the flowers appear from among the upper leaves, the whole forming a handsome plume. Only about ten species are known and one of the finest is *M. hirta,* with red and yellow flowers, which grows at Cape Point in situations exposed to the full storm blasts of the southern ocean. Fourteen genera of Proteaceae with some 350 species grow in South Africa and nearly all are meritorious plants but I have only space to mention one more, namely *Leucospermum nutans.* This, as I saw it, is a sparingly branched shrub from 3 to 5 feet tall with relatively short, broad leaves and terminal heads of brilliant red and orange-colored flowers suggesting a glorified shrubby Sweet Sultan with nodding flowers.

CHAPTER VI.
Heather-bells

IN ELEGANCE, beauty and wealth of blossoms Cape Heaths are not excelled by any group of shrubs the world over. Their loveliness is fascinating; their charm irresistible; their variety seemingly infinite; and every month of the year finds them bearing flowers in thousands. In size they vary from prostrate mats to sturdy bushes from 5 to 10 feet tall and as much in diameter. They are mostly social plants and, like their near relative the Heather of Scotland's moors often clothe acres and square miles of the countryside. They grow on sandy flats, in swampy places and on bleak, rock-strewn mountain slopes. Their clustered, multicolored flowers are of every hue and often each flower combines two or more color-schemes. In many the stamens are prominent and conspicuously colored. In size the flowers vary from tiny bells or urns each no larger than a pin's head to tubes an inch and more long. Some have the flowers clustered at the ends of the shoots; in others the flowers clothe nearly the whole of the current season's growth.   All have small leaves and twiggy branches, and are extraordinarily floriferous.   These we may consider generic characters, but in diversity of form and in color of flowers Mother Nature has frollicked with the Cape Heaths as with no other genus of shrubs.   Certain districts, such as the Cape promontory, Caledon, Riversdale and George, are especially famous for their variety of Heaths but to me it seemed that these plants luxuriated everywhere in the coastal region whilst not a few were happy under the drier conditions of the contiguous plateau.   My visit to the Cape happened in the autumn—the off season for Heaths—yet I collected in blossom more than 100 species and saw millions of plants laden with flowers. A scientist must not gush, and with the task of discoursing on flowers at large I have to be particularly careful in the use of superlatives, but the strongest in our language—or any language—would not exaggerate the beauty of the Heaths of the Cape of Good Hope.

To the garden-lover of from fifty to 100 years ago Cape Heaths made the Cape famous.   He knew, admired and grew these plants to perfection in the crudely heated greenhouses of the day.   In Andrews' four-volume work entitled "Heaths," published

1802-30, colored plates of 288 species and varieties are given. All are drawn from plants which flowered in the British Isles. One nursery firm, that of Messrs. Lee and Kennedy of Hammersmith, grew 228 kinds and these are listed by Andrews.

With the decline of indoor gardening in Europe, and of what little there ever was in this country, and the specialization which has increased so greatly with the development of modern greenhouses, Cape Heaths—except a few of the toughest sorts—have become lost to gardens. Never the easiest of subjects to successfully grow in pots they required skillful handling and more attention than the modern gardener either could or would give, and this as much as a change of fashion caused their wholesale disappearance from northern conservatories. In California the few species remaining thrive luxuriantly out-of-doors and had gardens flourished in the neighborhood of San Francisco half a century ago we should not have to deplore the loss of the Heaths of the Cape. In Bailey's "Cyclopedia" thirteen Cape species of Erica are enumerated and a dozen others with several hybrids are mentioned in small type. This emphasizes the poverty of our gardens.

Of the few now grown *E. melanthera* with small

white tinged with pink flowers each with prominent black anthers is perhaps the most common. Others are *E. ventricosa* with flowers of varied colors, *E. formosa* with white, *E. persoluta* and *E. hiemalis* with pink and white flowers. The last-named is probably a form of *E. perspicua*. The yellow-flowered *E. Cavendishiana* and *E. Wilmoreana*, with pink, tipped white, flowers, are of hybrid origin.

The first Cape Heaths introduced into cultivation were *E. marifolia* and *E. concinna*, seeds of which were received at Kew from Masson in 1773. The first-named grows a foot high and has relatively broad short leaves in verticils and terminal clusters of small white, urn-shaped flowers. It blossoms from April to July. The other grows 3 feet tall, has small leaves, tubular rose and white flowers in verticils on the shoots and is in blossom from October to December. The yellow *E. lutea,* still common on Table Mountain, the white and pink flowered *E. persoluta* and the bright scarlet *E. cerinthoides* with several others were introduced by Masson in 1774.

The distribution of the genus Erica is interesting. It is absent from America, Asia and Australasia. Several species are found in Europe from Britain south but more especially in the Mediterranean region, and these are known generally as Hardy Heaths. A few species occur on the higher mountains of Africa, both in the north and in the equatorial regions, but the real wealth and exuberance is reserved for South Africa where over 500 species are known and nearly all from the Cape Province.

CHAPTER VII.

Nature's Freaks and Fancies

UCCULENT plants are usually looked upon as the curiosities of the Vegetable World. The modifications of leaves and stems, whereby they serve as reservoirs largely for the storage of water, and the peculiar external tissues which aid in this conservation, give them a remarkable appearance. The principal regions of the world where succulents grow naturally are Mexico, the adjacent southwestern United States and South Africa. Each has its own types but superficially the plants look much alike.

The Cacti and Agaves of America have Euphorbias and Aloes with their relatives as their South African analogues. The species of Aloe are legion. A majority of them are low plants with one or few unbranched stems, many form an assemblage of stems and may be termed bushes, a few, like *A. ciliaris*, are scandent and several are tall trees. Their leaves are brittle and easily broken and are filled with sap containing a bitter principle; they are usually armed along the margin and are often curiously mottled and barred. All have handsome orange to scarlet flowers

which are produced in great profusion and the South
African Aloes in blossom are one of the floral sights
of the world. The giants of the family are *A.
Bainesii* and *A. dichotoma* which have branching
stems and are often from 30 to 40 feet tall. A good
many species are in cultivation and those who garden
in the warm dry parts of this country would be well
advised to add increasingly these plants to their collections. Where the climate is to their liking they
require little or no attention.

The succulent Euphorbias are also very numerous
and may be anything from nests of knobby stems a
few inches high to much-branched, candelabriform
trees 40 feet tall. Their inflorescences are insignifi-
cant and their stems contain a white juice which has
strong irritant and vesicatory, if not poisonous,
properties. Many of them are armed with ferocious
spines. On account of their repellent qualities they
have been much planted by the natives of Africa as
hedges to protect their kraals and villages from sur-
prise attacks by enemies. A number of species, doubtless as curiosities, were long ago introduced by Arab
traders into India and from there the Chinese carried
them to south China. In many parts of India and
China these plants today serve as hedges to fence in
homesteads.

Stapelia and Huernia are tufted plants with short, succulent. angular, knotty stems. Most of the species, and there are a great number, have more or less star-shaped flowers mottled and barred with blackish-brown or purple and emit an offensive carrion-odor. They attract flies of all sorts and these insects lay their eggs in the flowers and at the same time effect fertilization. The flowers vary from one-half to 2 inches in diameter but those of *Stapelia grandiflora* are fully 6 inches across, pale without, blackish purple and bearded on the inner surface.

Abundant and beautiful in blossom are the Mesembryanthemums of South Africa. They are a feature of the Karroo, where they cover large tracts. In their vegetative characters they exhibit a very wide range of variation. Some are much-branched little bushes, others sprawl on the ground with stems many yards long; others are cushion-like with two or three short, thick, spreading leaves raised a few inches above the earth or erect and buried with just their summit flush with the soil surface and look for all the world like small pebbles. So great is the similarity that when not in blossom the most argus-eyed person cannot distinguish between vegetable and rock substances on the Karroo. In those species which have erect. thick, fleshy leaves below ground the apex of the leaf, which is on a level with the soil surface, is of colorless tissue. These transparent layers of cells protect the leaf from loss of moisture and at the same time admit light freely to the green coloring matter contained in the tissues beneath. In short, they are windows protecting the chlorophyll grains from extremes of temperature and allowing these bodies to look at the sun by day and the star-lit heavens by night. The flowers of these peculiar plants are from three-fourths to 1½ inches across, white, yellow or pink, which perched upon short stalks appear to be independent of any plant and dot the desert as little stools of color on all sides.

Succulent plants belong to many genera and there are hundreds of species but I must conclude with mention of *Rochea falcata* and *R. coccinea*, well-known old garden plants which among other places flourish on Table Mountain. The first-named has pale gray, fleshy, 6-inch long, sickle-shaped leaves and broad terminal heads of orange-red flowers each with conspicuous yellow anthers. The other has small green leaves crowded on the stems and terminal heads of scarlet flowers. Both favor rocky places and are particularly happy in niches in the vertical walls of rock, safe by their inaccessibility from wanton hands.

CHAPTER VIII.

Bulbs of a Thousand Kinds

OUTH AFRICA gave to our gardens the parents of the modern Gladiolus and for this alone has earned our lasting gratitude. No bulbous plant is more at home in this country, and none is more extensively grown, and none has more enthusiastic admirers than the handsome, arrogant Gladiolus. As a flower it needs no introduction nor encomium but that its native home is South Africa may be news to many readers.

The bulbous plants of South Africa have won for themselves the generic title of Cape bulbs, under which name they are known and admired wherever flowers are grown. None of them are properly hardy in New England though the well-known *Galtonia candicans* comes pretty near being so. But in the warmer parts of the country a great many can be grown out of doors and in California the majority would flourish like native plants. Of none, not even Gladiolus, have the full uses been made and many have been quite neglected. All are remarkable for the brilliancy of their flowers but not a few are shy

to blossom under gray northern skies. They miss
the hot sun of their native land which in the dry
season bakes the earth and ripens the bulbs. A
majority of them rest through the dry season bursting into flower at the end and make their growth
during the rains. It should be remembered that the
seasons are opposite to ours and that the rainy season
is that of winter in the western part and summer in
the eastern, northern and interior parts of South
Africa. Cape bulbs flourish and blossom best under
full exposure to the heavens; when bushes invade
their domain they flower sparsely or not at all until
fire destroys the scrub. Cracks and niches in
boulders and cliffs are favorite places for plants like
Nerine and there they luxuriate with the bulbs exposed or covered only by their own dried up foliage.

Most of the Cape bulbs are found in the drier,
rocky parts of South Africa but the Watsonias are
partial to acid soils and the different species of Gladiolus flourish under a variety of climatic conditions.
Certain species like G. *alatus*, G. *cuspidatus* and G.
angustus are confined to the western part of the Cape
where winter rains prevail, others like G. *purpureo-
auratus* and G. *dracocephalus* to Natal with its heavy
summer rains, a few, like G. *psittacinus* and G.
Saundersii, are common to both regions. Some, as

for example G. *cardinalis* and G. *splendens*, are native of those parts where the annual rainfall is fairly equally distributed but is not excessive. Lastly there is G. *primulinus*, a child of the mist, whose home on the banks of the Zambesi River is constantly bathed in spray from the wonderful Victoria Falls, which are 400 feet high and a mile wide. The species mentioned are the chief parents of the Gladiolus we know today. Lest anyone think that finality has been approached in the development of this popular flower I would remind the reader that there are more than eighty other species known to grow wild in South Africa.

Ixias and Sparaxis are popular Cape bulbs, of which there are many named sorts sold by dealers. A strange looking plant is *Ixia viridiflora* with livid green flowers each with a black centre and yellow anthers larger than the black filaments. The spike is often more than a foot long and there are forms with pale blue and lilac-colored flowers. *Ixia maculata* has yellowish and *I. ovata* dark red flowers. Of Sparaxis there are many garden kinds descendant from the wild species, *S. tricolor*, which has flowers of many shades of color. An allied plant is the Wandflower, *Dierama ensifolium* often called *Spar-*

axis pulcherrima, with white, pink and purple flowers and known in Natal as Grassy-bells.

Pleasing little plants with plaited leaves and richly colored flowers are the Babianas, so-called because baboons are fond of their bulbs. A variable species is *B. stricta* with white, lilac-blue to pale yellow flowers; the variety *rubrocyanea* has red and blue flowers. Another (*B. plicata*) has violet-blue, clove-scented flowers. Less known is *B. ringens* with handsome scarlet flowers irregular in form, gaping at the mouth and much frequented by honey-loving birds.

With the genus Tritonia the hybridist has been busy in recent years and under the name of Montbretias the product is much grown in gardens. They are lovely plants with branched arching sprays carrying many yellow, orange, and red shading to crimson flowers from August to October. They love the sun and are almost hardy in Massachusetts. The Davison and Earlham hybrids are really wonderful plants and one named His Majesty is acclaimed the last word in Montbretias. The wild parents are chiefly *Tritonia aurea, T. crocosmiflora, T. crocata* and *T. Pottsii,* all common plants in South Africa.

Antholyza, of which there are several species, is very closely related to Gladiolus differing only in the

abrupt expansion of the flower-tube. A common
species at the Cape is *A. Merianella* with 18-
inch high stems carrying half-a-dozen bright orange-
colored flowers, each with a narrow tube and abruptly
dilated mouth. To the brilliancy of its blossom it
owes its common name of "Flames." *Antholyza
nervosa* has orange-red and *A. revoluta* bright red
flowers. All are showy plants worthy of more attention than they now receive in gardens.

Rivals of the Gladiolus in stateliness and beauty of
blossom are the Watsonias. With flower-spikes from
3 to 5 feet tall either simple or branched and bearing
dozens of large salmon, rose or flesh-colored Gladi-
olus-like flowers these plants are conspicuous in the
peaty areas of many parts of South Africa. The
most common species is *W. rosea* of which there is a
lovely white variety known as *Ardernei*. Frequent
also is *W. Meriana* whose stem bears several large
inflated sheaths which collect and hold water, and
many a traveller has quenched his thirst from these
reservoirs in times of drought. In Australia a fine
race of hybrids named *W. Croninii* has been raised
with tall branching stems and flowers of pure white
and delightfully pink shades of color. Other races
have been raised in Florida and in California and it is

my belief that Watsonia has a bright future before it in warm, temperate lands.

A genus of beautiful Cape bulbs which is now coming into popular favor is Nerine or Guernsey Lily. There are about a dozen species and a great many hybrids with white, pink, orange-red to fiery scarlet flowers. They blossom in the late autumn and early winter, sending up rigid stems a foot to a foot and a half tall which terminate in an umbel of from ten to twenty flowers, each 6-partite with recurving and often undulate segments and bright colored outthrust stamens. The colors are singularly pure and the flowers glisten and sparkle like diamonds. Some species flower from the naked bulbs, others produce new leaves, rich green or glaucous, and flower-spikes at the same time. One of the oldest known is *Nerine sarniensis* of which there are several varieties with flowers varying in color from salmon to fiery scarlet. Another old favorite is *N. Fothergillii major* with fine crimson-red flowers, and handsome is the newer *N. Bowdenii* with large pink blossoms, each segment with a dark medial line. A small greenhouse filled with Nerines in blossom, their flowers glistening and scintillating in the sun, is a splendid sight but picture acres of a countryside studded with these plants in full bloom and you have a glimpse of Nerines in a natural state in South Africa. North of the Orange River in shallow depressions which are occasionally flooded by rain water the beautiful *N. lucida* grows in immense numbers. The flowers are larger than in other species, pink in color and are produced with or immediately before the leaves. This plant deviates somewhat in structure from other Nerines in having a flattened stem and a slightly irregular flower with the six parts not quite free at the base. Discovered and introduced more than 100 years ago by the traveller, Burchell, and by him named *Amaryllis lucida* it was figured in the "Botanical Register" in 1820 as *A. laticoma* but does not appear to ever have been common in cultivation.

In England especially the hybridist has been busy with these charming bulbs and a large number of splendid named sorts are to be obtained from dealers. In Massachusetts where Nerines thrive as cool greenhouse plants there are several fine collections about which the flower-loving public is destined soon to hear. Cut Nerine flowers last long and there is an increasing demand for them.

In delightful fragrance no bulbous plant surpasses the old-time favorite *Freesia refracta alba* with its white tubular flowers borne from ten to twelve to-

gether at the end of slender stalks. There is a newer
form (*major*) with larger and more numerous
flowers. Another species (*F. Leichtlinii*) has yellow
and another (*Armstrongii*) rose-colored flowers.
From these the hybridist has produced a race with
vari-colored blossoms some of which are exquisite.
Buttercup, Treasure and Apogee are among the best
yellows; Amethyst and Merry Widow have soft
lavender to pale violet colored blossoms; in Rosa
Bonheur the flowers are pink with a yellow throat
whilst in Wistaria, one of the newest of these crea-
tions, the color is that of the famous vine after which
it is named. Freesias are of easy culture either from
seeds or bulbs and the flowers last for a long time
filling the whole house with a delightful and peculiar
perfume.

Another genus with which the hybridist in recent
years has wrought wonders is Lachenalia, the Cape
Cowslip. There are a score or more species known
but only a few of them are in cultivation. But fortunately these include *L. Nelsonii* and *L. tricolor*, two
of the best. The first-named has golden yellow and
the other green, scarlet and yellow tubular flowers.
The leaves are fleshy and the flowers are strung many
together on erect stalks; they are splendid subjects for
pans or baskets, blossoming freely in the early spring.

A species with red flowers is *L. pendula* which has the additional merit of blossoming at Christmas time. Among the hybrids Cawston Gem and Rector of Cawston and the new Excelsior Seedling have foot-high stalks carrying from twenty to thirty flowers of a deep yellow color tinged with red at the margins.

An old fashioned Cape bulb now-a-days not often seen is *Vallota purpurea,* the Scarborough Lily. This produces large handsome Amaryllis-like flowers of varying shades of scarlet and crimson from July to October, at the end of stalks from 1 to 2 feet tall. There is only one species but a number of forms, differing in color and size of the flowers, have received names. Vallota like Nerine, Crinum and other true bulbous plants of South Africa dislike interference and blossom most freely when long established in pots, pans or borders.

A stately group of bulbous plants are the Crinums, a genus of wide distribution in America, Asia and Africa and of which the Cape furnishes two or three of the hardiest and best species. The commonest South African species, fittingly named *Crinum capense,* bears from eight to twelve white or pink fragrant blossoms in an umbel at the head of a naked stalk 2 feet high. The Natal Crinum (*C. Moorei*) is somewhat similar with taller flower stems and rose-pink flowers. Hardier, more beautiful and a better garden plant than either is the hybrid C. *Powellii* with tall flower stems, ample lustrous foliage and lovely rose-colored or white, funnel-form, delightfully fragrant flowers. The garden value of these Crinums never has been fully appreciated. Their long-tubed goblet-like flowers rival Lilies in their exquisite shape, color and fragrance. The long, graceful rich green leafage is ornamental the summer long and the plants have a decided tropical luxuriance about them.

Very remarkable in flower are the different species of Brunsvigia or Spider-Lily. These have relatively small reddish flowers on long red stalks which in some species radiate from a common center like the spokes of a wheel. The umbels are many flowered but the stems are short and as often as not the flowers lie on the ground and look like large red spiders. One of the most abundant is B. *multiflora* and I shall long remember seeing from a railway train the rather arid veldt studded with its odd-looking spider-like flowers. When the seeds are ripe the whole inflorescence becomes detached and rolls about in the wind like a wheel. A taller growing species with flower stems 2 feet high and scarlet blossoms is B. *Joseph-*

ineae. Another species with pink blossoms in a rounded umbel is *B. toxicaria* whose bulb is very poisonous.

Curious also is the related genus Buphane with an inflorescence suggesting a hedgehog rolled into a ball with spiney quills poised erect. The common species are *B. ciliaris* with a loose head of a hundred small flowers on slender stalks and *B. disticha* with a compact of many-flowered mass of blossoms borne on a short stem arising from an enormous shaggy bulb.

Extraordinary are the Haemanthus or Blood Lilies with intense red-colored blossoms crowded at the end of a naked stalk, and standing boldly erect look like glowing balls, startling the unwary in the belief that they are the heads of fierce and dangerous reptiles. The head of flowers is surrounded by large fleshy colored bracts and the flower stem is striped and blotched with red-purple. Altogether about thirty species are known. The most common are *H. coccineus* with short mottled and *H. tigrinus* with striped flower-stalks, both having scarlet flowers with prominent yellow-anthered stamens.

One of the best known and most hardy of Cape bulbs is *Galtonia candicans* with pure white, fragrant dropping bells from fifteen to twenty on a naked stalk. A relative is *Pseudogaltonia Pechnelii* which has a flattened umbellate head of pendent green and white flowers and a bulb covered with bristly fibres. An old garden favorite is *Ornithogalum thyrsoides*, with broad pyramidate inflorescences of milk-white flowers. Known in South Africa as the Chinkerichee this is a sinister plant, all parts of it being poisonous to stock even when dry. There are other species of which I may mention *O. Thunbergianum* with handsome, rich yellow flowers.

Albuca, Bulbine, Urginea and Veltheimia have many representatives all rather weedy in appearance. Massonia is a curious genus of which mention may be made of *M. pustulata* with a dense head of whitish flowers raised above a couple of broad platter-like leaves. Yet another plant may be enumerated in *Tulbaghia violacea* which has grass-like leaves and clustered heads of purple flowers all strongly impregnated with the odor of garlic.

There are many, very many other Cape bulbs but I am not attempting finality. This chapter began with mention of the familiar Gladiolus, it may well conclude with that of the superb Belladonna Lily. This jewel with large pale to rose-pink funnel-form flowers, each flushed with yellow on the throat and borne many together in an umbel crowning a stout, naked stalk some 2 feet tall, is fortunately no stranger to garden-lovers. Adaptable and of easy culture it has made itself quite at home in our northern gardens. A common wild plant on the slopes of Table Mountain and elsewhere, *Amaryllis Belladonna* is a worthy product of a country, great and rich, destined to be the abiding home of millions of the white race —aptly named the Cape of Good Hope.

CHAPTER IX.

The First Harvesters

UCH was the fame of "Cape Plants" toward the end of the Eighteenth Century that when the Royal Gardens, Kew, decided to send out its first collector, the Cape of Good Hope was the region chosen. The object of the mission was the discovery of new plants for the improvement of the Royal Gardens. Francis Masson, one of his Majesty's gardeners, was selected for the work at a yearly salary of about $500 and expenses not to exceed $1,000 per annum. Sir Joseph Banks has left it upon record that Masson sent home a profusion of new plants which made Kew superior to every other European Botanic Garden.

Francis Masson, pioneer and forerunner of the many plant collectors sent out from the famous Kew Gardens, was born at Aberdeen, Scotland, in August, 1741. He reached the Cape in 1772, and on December 10th with oxen and cart and a Dutch guide, set out on his first journey. He travelled east as far as Swellendam, reaching it on January 18th, and then returned to Cape Town. At Stellenbosch he noted the row of large Oak trees on either side of the solitary street; the Hottentots Holland Mountains delighted him with their wealth of plants. On this journey seeds of many beautiful species of Erica, later raised and successfully grown at Kew, were collected. In September, 1773, accompanied by Carl Peter Thunberg, whose name is inseparably connected with early researches into the flora of South Africa and Japan, he carried out a journey eastward to Sundays River, where hostile Kaffirs necessitated their turning back. Cape Town was reached after an absence of four and a half months occupied in laborious and fatiguing travel.

On the journey many plants including *Protea grandiflora, Ixia viridiflora, Buphane disticha, Erythrina caffra, E. Humeana* and numerous Heaths were collected. He notes the fruitful nature of the country in many places, especially the Drakenstein region, and is impressed with the infinite variety of plants. On the mountains near Kaffir Kuils River, Masson found *Aloe succotrina* forming large clumps from 5 to 6 feet high and remarks that the peasants make great quantities of gum-aloes from the leaves, which they sell at the Cape for sixty cents a pound. On September 26, 1774, he set out on a third journey and a few days later was again joined by Thunberg. They travelled through part of the Karroo, which is described as an extraordinary tract of land in great want of fresh water, coming back to the Cape on December 28th after great hardships and sufferings from thirst. On this journey Masson collected a hundred new species and was much enamoured with the Stapelias, Euphorbias, Mesembryanthemums, *Aloe dichotoma* and other succulents.

In 1774, Masson returned to England and in 1776 was sent by Sir Joseph Banks to the West Indies where misfortune dogged his steps. Most of his collections were lost at sea. When the French attacked Grenada, Masson was called upon to bear arms in its defence and was taken prisoner fighting in the trenches. From 1786 to 1795, he was again in South Africa. Afterward he lived in England for a few years but, tiring of this inactive life, he journeyed to America, to die at Montreal in December, 1805, or January, 1806.

Masson introduced into Kew forty-seven species of Pelargonium and over 400 new species of plants. He is commemorated by the genus Massonia, named for him by Linnaeus, and by many species of Cape plants. The results of Masson's labors adorn the gardens of both hemispheres; his portrait hangs on a wall in the Linnaean Society's rooms in London and his mortal remains repose in an unmarked tomb in a

Montreal cemetery. It has been my privilege to traverse in South Africa much of the country visited by Masson and to gather specimens of many of the plants which he and Thunberg first made known to the world. On the Hottentots Holland Mountains in March, 1922, I plucked specimens of the lovely *Erica Massonii*—scarlet, viscid flowers tipped with yellow and green—and thrilled with delight similar to that which the discoverer himself must have experienced when he first saw this exquisite gem. To me this plant, beautifying the rock-strewn mountain slopes, seems a fitting memento of one whose life was spent in garnering material with which to beautify the gardens of the northern world.

The first Englishman to collect at the Cape seems to have been George Stonestreet, who flourished about 1695 and sent plants to Plukenet from the Cape and also from India.

Another pioneer who did splendid work was Joseph Niven. He collected in South Africa for George Hibbert and the Empress Josephine from 1798 to 1803, and from 1803 to 1812, for Messrs. Lee and Kennedy, a famous nursery firm of the period. Niven learned to speak the Kaffir language perfectly and on this account was forced to accompany the British troops in the Kaffir War as guide and interpreter. for which service he received neither recognition nor reward. He returned to England in disgust and in 1826 died in his native village, Pennicuik, near Edinburgh, at the age of fifty-four. He is commemorated by Nivenia, a genus of fine Proteaceous plants.

The well-known *Sparmannia africana* is named for Anders Sparrman, a Swedish naturalist, who visited South Africa in 1772 and again in 1775-6. That fine red-flowered shrub *Burchellia capensis* recalls a famous traveller and naturalist, John William Burchell, who was in South Africa from 1811-15. The remarkable *Gardenia Thunbergii* was introduced into England in 1773 by Sir James Cockburn. The gigantic *Aloe Bainesii* with branching stems and swollen trunk-base and the extraordinary *Welwitschia Bainesii,* which although it lives for centuries never produces more than the first two leaves, were discovered by Thomas Baines, who came to the Cape in 1842, died in Durban in 1875 and occupied the post of artist in the Second Kaffir War. The curious *Bowiea volubilis,* a poisonous plant with an onion-like bulb and fleshy twining stems rather suggesting a kind of Asparagus, was named by Harvey in memory of James Bowie, a second Kew collector to the Cape. Bowie in 1814-16 had accompanied the fa-

mous Allan Cunningham to Brazil and was sent to
the Cape where he collected from 1817-22. He returned there in 1827 with the intention of making a
business of collecting and remained in South Africa
the rest of his life. He introduced many plants, including the useful *Streptocarpus Rexii*, that striking Cycad, *Encephalartos horridus*, and the fine *Clivia no-
bilis*. This last came from the neighborhood of
Grahamstown but for "prudential business reasons"
Bowie reported it from the Orange River! Bowie
seems to have been an odd character, cherished his
wrongs, real and imaginary, became embittered and
outcast and died in poverty in 1869. Named at the
request of Bowie, *Streptocarpus Rexii* commemorates George Rex, a notable character, and a natural
son of George III of England and Hannah Lightfoot,
a Quakeress. As a young man, Rex was sent out to
South Africa well endowed with cash and an injunc-
tion that he was never to return to England. At
first he occupied some minor official post and lived in
Capetown, but when the Cape again passed from
British to Dutch control he, with others of British
descent, were forced to leave. Journeying westward
he came to Knysna where he settled and subsequently
died. He appears to have been a man of considerable
ability and force of character but, like so many others

of his day, very loose living and many of his descendants now are markedly colored.

Scores of other travellers and collectors have added their quota to the sum of our knowledge of Cape plants but there is no space to pursue further this subject. As in other parts of the world so, too, in South Africa it is to many men of high and low degree—some commemorated, but a greater number neglected and unknown—that we owe the many plants that so notably embellish our gardens.

CENTRAL AFRICA

CHAPTER X.

A Happy Hunting Ground

HE part of interior Africa best known to Americans is beyond doubt Kenya Colony astride the Equator. Even before the late Theodore Roosevelt of immortal memory visited the region in quest of big game it was known to many American sportsmen. And since that time it has become the mecca of the big game hunter and every year welcomes visitors from this country. Although the herds of game are today less enormous than formerly the region boasts both variety and quantity greater than any other part of the earth. That herds of this game may be known to posterity a vast preserve has been set aside forever and hunting is properly controlled by license. To the sportsmen of all nations it is and for all time will be a happy hunting ground. But Kenya is much more than this. It is largely highland country enjoying a salubrious climate and is the only equatorial region of the earth where white men have a fair chance of founding permanent homes. It possesses huge tracts of pastoral and arable lands and wide forests rich in useful timber trees.   In its rich valleys excellent coffee is produced and on the uplands flax and wheat-growing and the industry of dairying are firmly established.   Favored by climate Kenya is destined to serve the white man's needs and comforts far beyond the capabilities of other tropic lands. Brought under British influence in 1887 and created a Crown Colony in 1920 peace and order reign where not fifty years ago the slave-trader plied his nefarious traffic.

Africa has been likened to an inverted dish, that is to say the interior is a vast plateau approached from the coast by a series of about three narrow, rather abrupt steps.   The breadth of each step varies somewhat according to the point of approach, but nowhere on the Indian Ocean side is it considerable. The plateau in altitude ranges from 5000 to 9000 feet above sea-level.   A few mountains rear themselves above the general level and almost athwart the Equator there are ancient volcanic ranges nearly 20,000 feet high whose peaks carry glaciers and snow eternal.

Another and even more remarkable feature of Africa's topography is a great rift or valley some 5000 feet deep whose bed is filled with many long narrow lakes. Of volcanic origin and caused by sinkage this depression extends more or less interruptedly from Portuguese East Africa northward, includes the Red Sea, and, crossing to Asia Minor, the Dead Sea and the Valley of Jordan. The rolling downs of the Kenya highlands terminate in a gigantic escarpment of volcanic rock that overhangs this great rift, but of the volcanoes that poured their lavas over these uplands only the highest peaks have withstood the erosive action of time.

The highlands of Kenya are easily reached by a metre-gauge railway from Mombasa on the shores of the Indian Ocean. A night's journey from that torrid town and the cool of approaching uplands is apparent and within twenty-four hours the capital town, Nairobi, is reached. Here on the very edge of the highlands one sleeps under a blanket every day in the year. The region takes its name from a jagged peak situated just south of the Equator and at three degrees south stands the still higher Kilimanjaro Mountain with a dome-shaped summit. These snow-clad equatorial mountains rank among the wonders of the world. From the plains near Nairobi, when the atmosphere is clear, they may be seen towering into the heavens, unearthly, uncanny, magical.

Vast areas of the rolling uplands of Kenya are

clothed with grass where the herds of game find food in abundance.   Here the wandering Masai roams with his cattle which he counts his sole wealth. Until recently this warrior race spread terror on every side, slaughtering and enslaving the tribes he came in contact with.   Having found in the white man a greater warrior than himself the Masai accepts the situation and contents himself with amassing droves of cattle and roaming free where he wills.   With his long spear ever present in his arms he is to be seen from the railway trains on the plains and at the stations.   So, too, are his chubby smiling females with their arms, ankles and necks swathed in bands of wire which they favor as ornaments of rare value.   No longer living in daily fear of marauding, murdering Masai, the Kikuyu and Kavarondo tribes addicted to agriculture live in peace and tend their crops and homes. They dislike paying a hut-tax, the only collectible tax possible, and prefer to work only when fancy dictates but I found them to be a cheerful, happy-go-lucky folk, worth-while knowing.

I was attracted to Kenya not by its wealth in big game but by what I had learned from sportsmen about its trees and flowers.   In America, Red Cedars are familiar trees, useful, ornamental and picturesque though never of more than ordinary size.   In Kenya the giant of the race has its home and it was to see and know this tree that I journeyed. A well-fitted steamer decently crowded with interesting passengers took me from Bombay to Mombasa and the train puffing and panting set me down at Nairobi in November, 1922. Hospitality and Kenya I found to be synonymous. A few inquiries and I was armed with the information necessary for the task I had in hand and set out on the quest in exuberant spirits. And I knew no others during my subsequent travels over much of Africa.

There is ever a lure in mountains no matter where situated. They draw one irresistibly to their summits and nowhere does the heart of man beat more joyously than on some lofty eminence. First there is the mystery of the mountains. What do their solitudes boast and what shall I find are temptations that few can resist. Then comes the struggle upward, one's will to conquer pitted against nature's obstacles drives one on. 'Tis battle against elemental forces and success is sweet, sweet indeed. The greater the struggle the sweeter the fruits of victory. Summit attained at last, winded, exhausted probably, nothing but a sea of rocks in view save the heavens above and yet what mountaineer would barter his victory for wages in gold? Primitive instincts prevail and conquest is sufficient reward.

In a lifetime of travel in many lands the lure of the mountain peaks has often seized me, obsessed me, drawn and driven me to the summits. Often have I taken myself to task, called myself names and made bold resolutions only to break them as others do on the first occasion.

Pausing to rest on some high land on the outskirts of Nairobi as evening approached I saw floating on the distant horizon to the southward the rounded mass of Kilimanjaro. To the north the jagged peaks of Kenya speared the heavens. Remote, isolated, cleaving the blue vault these majestic volcanic peaks looked no real part of the world on which I stood. Their image registered on my brain floats before me as I write and I feel now as then, glad that I have lived and seen these monarchs of Africa's distant land.

The lure tugged violently at the heart strings but for once was strangled for limited time forbade any attempt to visit such distant peaks. As solace I treated myself to the ascent of the 12,500-foot Aberdare range and vastly enjoyed it. The climb came about quite legitimately if unexpectedly. Since it was necessary to get acquainted with the forest limits

in Kenya, I argued that there was no harm in finding
out what the flowers were like that grew a thousand
feet or so above the forests. A natural inquisitive-
ness I suffer from was all in favor of the argument
and decided the question in the affirmative. "Who
knows what queer growth fashions itself on the
equator's narrow belt," said the voice. "Go, of
course you must go and find out." So I went as my
story tells.

First, however, I sought my gigantic Red Cedar
(*Juniperus procera*), found him, caressed him,
photographed him bole and branch, gathered specimens of him, slept beneath him and begged his
friendship in ways known best to tree-lovers. For
two weeks I lived with him and was introduced to
a great many of his tree friends. I could tell of the
handsome *Pygeum africanum* with red mahogany-
like wood, of fragrant African Camphor (*Ocotea
usambarensis*) useful Milanje Podocarp (*Podocarpus milanjiana*) and handsome Yellow-wood (*P.
gracilior*), tough Olives (*Olea chrysophylla* and *O.
Hochstetteri*), whose wood supplies the railway
engines with fuel, and many others, including the
enormous Fig (*Ficus Hochstetteri*) of subtle, de-
vastating habits who starts life on the breast of a
hospitable neighboring tree and later strangles it

within the folds of its own huge bulk. Yes, much
did I learn in Red Cedar's company but I must content myself here with an account of my intimate
friend whose wood is now being used in America
for making pencils. His picture depicts his gigantic
size. At maturity he stands from 100 to 150 feet
tall with a straight, often fluted trunk from 20 to
30 feet in girth, clean of branches of 60 feet or so,
then spreads large branches into a rounded or flattened crown. Starting life as a compact pyramidal
growth of green or grey-green and not unlike our
own Virginian Cedar, this African relative ultimately
dominates and lords it over the region in which he
makes his home. His wood is fragrant, straight of
grain and easily worked, lasting well both in and out
of ground. Its uses are many and for making the
useful writing pencil ranks next to the Cedars of
eastern North America. To this country and to
Europe the wood is imported for that purpose. My
friend the Cedar confided to me his troubles. Born
chieftain of his land he resented being crowded by
trees of less noble lineage, complained of their mur-
derous infanticide, although in many broad acres I
noticed that he ruthlessly destroyed trees that sheltered him when young and brooked no rival. He
also complained that some regions refused him suffi-

cient water to dissolve his food and nourish his roots. Ancient monarchs were listless under attacks of fungus-growth and when told that it was the natural result of dotage were not in the least comforted. But on the whole the chief complaint was of a Mistletoe, a tiny thing of a few inches that insisted on living on his branches, would not fend for itself nor be dislodged. Millions of these plants crowd, nestlike, the lofty crowns of my Cedar and work their mischievous will. I confess he has his troubles but in open country where sufficient water is available no tree can wrestle successfully with him and none excel him in beauty nor in stature, and his usefulness to man is very great. The white man who has stayed the warring of the Masai is turning his attention to my lordly Red Cedar and by proper forestry methods is intent upon insuring for him equal, nay favored, opportunity to flourish perpetually.

It was in the land of the soil-loving Kikuyu with genial Forester Munro that I sojourned with Red Cedar. From there I took a train to Naivasha with its receding lake of brackish waters and Masai herdsmen. Northward from this place I was bumped over rolling downs in an Overland car to Kinobop forestry station where I was the guest of big-hearted H. G. Deakin and of his charming, capable wife. On the way we disturbed herds of Zebra, Kongani and other antelopes and it was a pretty sight to watch these animals careering over the plains.

The altitude of the forestry station is about 9000 feet, behind and beyond it tower the Aberdare Mountains and in front the broad expanse of plain which we had traversed. The station boasted a fine garden in which European vegetables and flowers grew in abundance and perfection. A plentiful water-supply is provided by a nearby stream and in this irrigated virgin soil plants luxuriated. Nowhere have I seen finer Sweet Peas, Carnations, Stocks, Pansies and Madonna Lilies than in this remote spot.

From the station a broad path leads through scrub and a remnant of Red Cedar forest to a trail ascending the Aberdare Mountains. The climb is easy over a path which zigzags to the summit of the ridge some 3000 feet above the forest station. On the outskirts of the forest remnant, a tree, St. John's Wort (*Hypericum lanceolatum*), favorite nurse of the Red Cedar in babyhood, flaunted its rich yellow blossoms aplenty. At one point the trail passes through a broad belt of Bamboos whose stems are often 50 feet tall despite its name *Arundinaria alpina*. As a potential source of paper-pulp this alpine Bamboo is viewed with favor, the more so because of its vast quantity. At the moment, however, its interest to me was in the fact of its being the home of wild elephants whose acquaintance I did not wish to make. The trails they make in crashing through these Bamboo-brakes were many and my companion, Forester Deakin, told that somewhere northward in the forested valley is the lordly elephant's valhalla. It awaits discovery and the fortunate will find there rich wealth in ivory. But the giant pachyderm is a canny, nay, uncanny beast with subtle brain stored with secrets not known to man. My forester friend had pursued many trails but only odd tusks of little value had been his reward.

Cool air and brilliant sunshine made walking very pleasant and when tired we rode mule and pony. As we approached the gap which thereabouts marks the summit of the range cold invigorating air played boisterously around us. The gap reached, before us lay an undulating basin bounded by escarpments and clad with a general miscellany of bushes and herbs, and a few odd trees of no great size. Much of this basin is peat bog turfed with tussock sedges and grasses with brown water oozing and stagnating in and around. Here and there are sluggish streams and tarns. For some ten or more miles we traversed this basin to a hut built near a large pond for the use of those whose work had been the stocking of some nearby streams with trout.

The alpine vegetation of this upland basin, eroded, wasted crater of an ancient volcano, afforded me merry interest. Everything was new and strange. An odd Delphinium and Clematis, stragglers from a northern land, smiled welcome, the salmon-red flowered native *Gladiolus Makinderi* was inclined to be friendly and so too were yellow-blossomed Ragworts (Senecios). Tall blue and lavender-flowered Lobelias, stiff and stately, stared coldly at us but most of the plants positively frowned upon our intrusion. Blackest of all lowered a tree Heath (*Ericinella Mannii*) with dense, more or less pyramidal, billowy crown 30 feet tall and short trunk often 7 feet in girth. The tiny flowers of this curious tree are crowded among the minute leaves and each branch is a plume of blossom. The true Tree Heath (*Erica arborea*) has strayed from Spain and northern Africa to these equatorial mountains but is little better than a bush on the Aberdares although its wealth of white and pale pink blossoms makes it attractive.

The Lobelias are not lowly herbs or even vigorous perennials such as our Cardinal Flower but veritable trees with stout trunks and from 10 to 20 feet tall. Very common was *Lobelia Gregoriana* with bluish purple flowers standing stalwart in the glades and marshes. Even taller is *L. Telekii* with violet flowers protected by very long green bristles of odd appearance. The Ragworts, too, are trees sometimes 25 feet tall with trunks a foot in girth. A common and handsome sort is *Senecio keniensis* with large branching heads of rich yellow Daisy-like flowers surmounting a tuft of silvery grey tongue-like leaves each two feet long. These Senecios and Lobelias standing sentinel-like or in platoons are striking features of the landscapes.

Here and there grow groves of a curious tree which from a distance suggests the familiar Rowan of northern lands. It has a similar pinnate leaf but instead of red berries broad clusters of curious winged dry fruits hang down from the branches. It proved to be a giant relative of the lowly Alchemilla of northern waysides and waste places, named *Brayera anthelmintica* by botanists and Kimondo by the Kikuyus of Kenya. I like the native name best. The Kimondo at its best is a tree fully 50 feet tall, with a trunk 9 feet in girth and a flattened crown 40 feet through and is the most alpine tree in Kenya.

I have mentioned sedges and grasses and these have for companions thickets of low grey-green foliaged shrubs strongly like many of our Willows. A cursory examination showed that they were Africa's substitute but in no way related. On close scrutiny I detected here a red thread-like pistil and there a cluster of yellow-anthered stamens protruding from the axils of the upper leaves. I was baffled completely and it was months afterwards on Table Mountain overhanging Capetown that I learned their names. My Willow analogues of the Aberdares are Cliffortias, related to the Kimondo and both are strange aberrant members of the family we know best by the Rose!

While crossing the basin my companion's quick eye detected afar three Thomson's Gazelle, one of which, thanks to his unerring aim, provided both us and our dusky followers with a satisfying and savory meal.

As the sun dipped below the horizon the temperature rapidly declined also. We lodged about half a degree south of the Equator but at just over 11,000 feet altitude and were glad to hug a large fire in an open grate. Delightfully tired after a wonderful day we retired early and crowded on the blankets. About 3 A. M. my Good Fairy awakened me and told me to look outside. Obeying the voice I opened the door and stepped without. Amazement was mine. The moon was dipping on the horizon, the Milky Way hung a perfect arc immediately over my head, its glistening myriad stars shone with startling brilliancy, the darting facets of light of an intenseness that could be felt. So near they seemed that I could almost clutch them with upraised hands; the ground around was white with hoar frost which threw back the sparkling rays rippling with laughter. The earth, myself and all around me were enveloped in the ethereal glory of the star-set heavens. Not before nor since have I witnessed so sublime a spectacle as on the summit of the Aberdare range. And I murmured a prayer of thanks to the Good Fairy as shivering but elated I went inside the hut and crawled beneath my blankets.

CHAPTER XI.

Cradle of the Nile

HE Nile, the most wonderful of all rivers, and the known history of the human race are deeply entwined. Its lower reaches in Egypt have been known from earliest biblical times but its source was not discovered until July 28, 1862. Who first began the quest, or when, we do not know but the secret was wrested from the heart of Africa by Captain Speke. In my youth the discovery was common talk and I dreamed of some day visiting the source and viewing it with my own eyes. The dream was realized during the closing days of 1921 in quite a prosaic manner. Stepping off a 1200 ton steamer on to the jetty of Jinza a fifteen minute stroll brought me to the end of my rainbow. I sat on the edge of the Ripon Falls and watched the waters of the Victoria Nyanza tumble over a cliff and give birth to the River Nile. The holy Nile like the gods of old is born adult. No bubbling of some petty spring gives it birth, none but the waters of Africa's largest lake suffice. A rent in the rim of this lake three-quarters of a mile wide over which rushes some 500 cubic metres of water per second is the birthplace of this mighty river. Over a broad and rock-strewn bed the waters rush and tumble forward as if delighted to escape from the quiet of the vast equatorial basin that had collected and chained them. Cool and sparkling are these waters and forty-five-pound fish besport themselves on the very edge of the maelstrom at the foot of the falls. Two other falls hasten the waters' departure and as one gazes down the long vista of the new-born Nile it shows neither diminution nor increase in width.

Three rocky islets clad with shrubbery divide the sparkling waters of the Ripon Falls. The view is charming and the halo of sentiment crowning the spot creates feelings of awe and reverence. As fittingly becomes a pilgrim I descended to the river's edge, lay down and drank deep of the sweet waters. Later I sought the steamer which leaving in the evening landed me next day at Kisumu, where I took a train to Mombasa 584 miles distant across Kenya Colony.

The Victoria Nyanza is not only the greatest of African lakes but is the largest lake in the Old World. It is about 255 miles long by about 155 miles in width with a superficial area of 26,828 miles and its mean elevation is 3726 feet above sea-level. It was discovered by Speke from the south in 1858 and by Baker from the north in 1863. Its eastern shores were first visited in 1883 by Thomson. Nearly all other of the major African lakes are long and narrow and occupy volcanic rents but Victoria Nyanza is not only the largest of African lakes but is different in character, being merely a collection of waters contained in a shallow basin of vast size. It is nowhere very deep, some 270 feet being the greatest depth found. It has sinuous shelving shores, a multitude of small islands and its whole basin is steadily decreasing. There is nothing grand about its shores where I saw them for they are uninteresting grass and scrub plains merging into muddy shallow waters. The central body of this huge fresh-water lake is free of islands and sea-like in aspect and violent storms are not infrequent.

At Kisumu I boarded a neat up-to-date steamer one Sunday morning and found myself among a crowd of interesting folk. Clear tropic skies and calm waters favored the twenty-hour voyage to Entebbe in Uganda. Approaching the western shores many islands are seen, none of any great size but clad with green forests girdled by a silver strand on which clear waters lap, they look like bits of paradise. On enquiring I learned history sinister. These most alluring tropic isles were uninhabited. There abides the dreaded Tsetse fly, carrier of the sleeping sickness. This most fatal malady had scourged these islands from 1898 to 1906 and what inhabitants had escaped had been removed to the main land. During those years when the epidemic was at its height tens of thousands died and the whole population of the lake region decimated. I shuddered as I gazed and thought of my old friend Mahon, who contracted this disease when pioneering in the very port where I was about to land and died one of the first white victims of sleeping sickness. Everything known at the time to medical science had been done but after a two-year struggle the end came. A raw day in early spring with other friends I stood beside the grave in Richmond, Surrey, and cast a handful of earth on the casket that contained his wasted remains. These memories flooded my mind and yet these smiling islands and the cheerful shores of Uganda seemed to bid us hearty welcome. Also I found the welcome real and when the time to leave came was loath to depart.

That great African traveller, Stanley, in 1875 christened Uganda the "Pearl of Africa" and I found it so. Richly forested, well watered, capable of producing vast riches from cotton, coffee, cocoa and other tropical crops it has a great future. Its principal people, the Baganda, are the most intelligent of African communities and not unwilling to work. Under the strong protecting arm of Britain, tribal wars have been put down and peace rules. In 1890 the British East Africa Company took over Uganda but it proved too big a problem for the company and in 1893 Great Britain assumed the control.

In the parts of Uganda visited by me red laterite rocks prevailed and surprising was the extent of the most excellent roads. More than 500 miles of good automobile roads were open then and each year these are added to. A forester friend met me at Entebbe and later in the day whisked me in a Ford car over a smooth road to Kampala, the chief town. From Kampala another forester carried me in the side-car of his motor-cycle here, there and everywhere. I came to look over the vegetation, get some idea of what the country was like and thanks to the motor-cycle I accomplished vastly more than I had dreamed of doing.

The forests of Uganda accessible to me, though rich in variety are jungle like and impenetrable and I found them less interesting than those of Kenya Colony. On the mountains to the west and north a better type obtains but these were denied me. Near the lake I saw large areas of tall Papyrus Reed famous from Egyptian times. On the edges and in drier open country the prickly *Phoenix reclinata* Palm forms clumps and thickets. In other places the tall *Raphia monbuttorum* rears itself full 50 feet and bears huge hanging inflorescences. From the wide-spreading leaves of this Palm the nests of the Weaver Bird hang in great numbers with quaint effect. Tall Incense Trees (*Canarium Schweinfurtii*) and wide-crowned *Piptadenia africana* are features of the forests and here and there grows the Upas trees (*Antiaris toxicaria*). The legend of deadly poison-ous vapors emanating from this tree is known the world over. But it is merely a legend and a gross libel on a stately tree. The tree is perfectly innocuous but it frequently grows in deep valleys where hangs heavy carbonic-acid gas, deadly to man and animals alike—hence the origin of this myth. One other tree, *Kigelia aethiopica,* the Sausage-tree, may be men-tioned. This is a strange looking fellow, low of stature, with a wide-spreading crown strung in sea-son with bologna sausage-like fruits.

Since 1900 much attention in Uganda has been given to tropical agriculture and with good results. Coffee of sorts is indigenous there and in adjacent Kenya and coffee-growing has proved a successful industry. Cotton does splendidly and is one of the principal exports. Cocoa is promising and Sesamum flourishes. Sugar-cane does well; Maize and Bananas supply the natives with food.

Trees and vines yielding rubber of inferior quality are native of the forests and many exotic rubber-yielding trees have been planted in Uganda. A miscellaneous assortment of these trees line the main road from Kampala toward Entebbe, planted under the enthusiastic direction of a former Governor. In many parts of tropical Africa prior to and during the World War many extensive plantations of Para Rubber (*Hevea brasiliensis*) and Ceara Rubber (*Manihot Glaziovii*) were made. In Tanganyika, in the coastal regions of Kenya, as well as in Uganda, this had taken place, and what I am about to say applies equally to all three regions. Ceara rubber is not only inferior but the tree is a hopeless failure in east and central Africa. In Uganda, Para Rubber is expected to succeed, though I think the expectancy is based more on enthusiasm and hope than on practical knowledge. The rainfall is insufficient and the tree grows three times less rapidly there than in Ceylon, Malaya and Java. It costs anywhere from $7500 to $10,000 per acre to plant and for the life of me I cannot see what possible chance it has of competing with the product so much more cheaply, easily and quickly produced in equatorial Asia.

In recent months much has been heard about the high price of rubber and many schemes for increasing the sources of supply have been promulgated. Some have acclaimed Liberia on the west coast of Africa a promised land. Investors, beware. It is high-grade para rubber that the world demands. So far as experiments have been tried, and they have been many, tropical Africa and the Para Rubber-tree are not in accord. From the knowledge available there is little reason to hope that Africa can solve the rubber problem.

CHAPTER XII.

Smoke That Thunders

HERE they are, there they are!" excitedly shouted my fellow travellers on the train I had boarded sixteen hours before at Bulawayo as it toiled across the savannahs toward the Victoria Falls. Following their gaze I saw white plume-like clouds floating in the sky and knew that they were immense volumes of spray shot up from the famed Falls of the Zambesi River. The train was twelve to fifteen miles distant from the Falls but on calm days these clouds of spray in five columns are visible at propitious seasons from a distance of twenty-five miles. The natives call them "Mosi-oa-tunya," the smoke that thunders— a pleasing and appropriate name.

Soon above the noise of the train itself the rumble of the falls was heard which increased to a booming roar as the train pulled up at the Victoria Falls station. We disembarked and were quickly ensconced in the well-found hotel, built for the accommodation of visitors, one mile from the Falls and commanding a splendid view of the river, railway bridge and surrounding country. Here for a week, enjoying every luxury of western civilization and abounding courtesy, I loafed and revelled in the marvels of this unique natural phenomenon—the waters of a river a mile wide suddenly crashing 400 feet down a rent in the earth not 400 feet wide, and boiling out through a gap only 300 feet broad, to zigzag through a corkscrew gorge, flowing parallel to itself several times in a course of a few miles, and continuing its tortuous passage through forty miles of canyons, collectively known as the Batoka Gorge.

Above and below the Falls the country is of the same general level and about 3000 feet above the sea. It is open and park-like in appearance and is dotted with trees standing wide apart and each by itself. Below the Falls the river, a narrow channel, is hidden 400 feet down in a canyon walled in by vertical precipices. Above the Falls and almost level with the plain it flows a placid stream a mile wide whose blue bosom is studded with islets clothed with green forests. The towering volumes of spray and the thunderous noise mark the rent into which the waters disappear. Amazing, awesome, terrifying, yet transcendently noble in their grandeur are the Victoria Falls.

From no one point can the Falls in their full width be seen owing to the immense clouds of mist. Puffs of wind disclose that on the upper lip of the rent two islands are obtruded and here and there rugged masses of bare rock stand parting the falling waters. Standing on the lower lip of the rent, drenched in spray, deafened by the noise and hardly able to breathe, one sees the chasm filled with mists where hang superb rainbows, perfect circles, of a brilliancy unknown, even startling to us who know only northern latitudes; at night when the moon is up soft lunar rainbows illumine the scene.

Just below the Falls and within full reach of their spray the river, a seething cauldron of water, is spanned by an iron cantilever bridge some 650 feet long and 350 feet above the water level. Over this bridge passes the railway which extends far northward into the Belgian territory of the Upper Congo.

Fringing the Falls is a dense green forest, whose exuberant growth, due to the falling spray, stands out in relief against the open park-like character of the landscape in general. The Falls and their immediate vicinity are preserved as a park, paths have been laid out and seats provided for the comfort of guests. Clad in raincoats and high boots one may pursue a path through the forest of jungle-growth from the southern edge of the Falls to near the railway bridge. A pleasant walk is this among large trees, crowded with Mosses and Ferns, and huge climbers rambling over and among trees. Thick nests of a feathery-leaved Palm (*Phoenix reclinata*), a feature of wet places everywhere in Africa from the Equator to Natal, abound. On the outskirts of the fringe stand, either alone or in groups, specimens of the lofty fan-leafed Ivory Palm (*Hyphaene ventricosa*) whose globose brown fruits, each as large as an apple, furnish vegetable ivory. Strange Terminalias, Peltophorums, Copaiferas, thorny Acacias and other trees, some laden with blossoms and others with fruits, dot the savannah. Here and there an odd Maroola tree (*Sclerocarya caffra*), whose fruits and young shoots are favorite food of the elephant, is seen. Large tangled climbers with bright colored flowers abound with bushes and herbs. In early morning and evening the air is laden with pleasant scents floating on the fragrance of the falling waters.

Here and yonder stand gigantic Baobab trees whose bulk of trunk typifies Africa. Huge indeed are these smooth-barked monsters with short, massive, knotty branches. In the dry season when bare of foliage and its whole form exposed the Baobab is decidedly ugly, even repellent in appearance. Clad in its mantle of dark green leaves, each digitately divided into distinct leaflets like the Buckeye of

America, it arrests attention and commands respect even if it does not win admiration. The flowers are white, saucer-shaped, suggestive of Magnolia blossoms, fragrant and handsome. The fruit is singular, the shape of a very large egg, woody in texture, clothed with soft tawny brown hairs and hangs suspended from a long stalk; the interior is filled with a white powder tasting like cream-of-tartar, in which the seeds are imbedded. Peculiar to Africa this bulky uncouth giant tree is symbolical of the continent, outwardly austere yet tender of heart. Every traveller from the very earliest tells of this tree and on an island immediately above the Falls the great Scotch Missionary traveller, David Livingstone, carved his initials on a Baobab tree when he discovered and named the Victoria Falls in 1855. On another tree, which is 90 feet in girth at its base, and grows about two miles from the hotel, five hundred and more subsequent visitors have been guilty of like offense but without the missionary's pardonable excuse. Like the smooth-barked Beech of our northern lands the Baobab in Africa is an irresistible lodestone to anyone possessed of a knife.

Now-a-days there is little game in the immediate neighborhood of the Falls. In the wet forests an occasional Pookoo antelope may be surprised. In the river itself Hippopotami occur at times in good numbers and Crocodile, too, rapacious, ugly fellows of sinister and ruthless character. Fish of various sorts offer good sport to the followers of Isaac Walton and in the waters below the Falls Tiger-fish and Gorge-fish are prizes worthy of a sportsman. Birds of many kinds are frequent and soaring overhead or at rest on the bare branches of the loftiest trees, the handsome white-headed Fish Eagle may be seen. The iron horse has brought the comforts and amenities of western civilization to the heart of Africa; life and property are safe and dainty ladies from America and Europe visit and take pleasant walks where twenty-five years ago only hunters ventured among the warring savages that disputed with the lordly game for the possession of the region. Except that the game has mostly departed, the region has not changed neither have its beauties been diminished. The railway does not wantonly obtrude neither does the low well-built hotel, which from a distance suggests a large country mansion set in its own park land. The bridge alone stands conspicuous but no one can quarrel with the outlines of this masterpiece of engineering. Did the spirit of its discoverer return one thinks he would be satisfied with what has happened since the white man took over dominion.

That greatest of all African hunters, the late Frederick C. Selous of undying memory, summing up the scenery and grandeur of the Victoria Falls wrote, "One of, if not the most transcendently beautiful natural phenomena on this side of Paradise." As I roamed among the scenes Selous' tribute floated across my memory and my heart responded fervently, "Amen."

On the nether lip of the rent into which the waters of the Zambesi plunge and jutting out into the breach through which the maddened waters surge and boil 400 feet below is Danger Point. It is treeless and boggy, clothed with sedges and grasses and is perpetually bathed in spray. Alluring as such dangerous places are. I plunged into the mists and bogs to obtain the nearest view of the Falls. The inrush of air is such that breathing is difficult and audible speech impossible. On this adventure I surprised my first *Gladiolus primulinus* in full blossom or, rather, it surprised me. On this point, and adjacent spray drenched areas, this charming flower grows aplenty and from the Victoria Falls it came to western lands. Beyond the range of the descending spray I saw only occasional plants. It loves the drenched areas, standing erect its flower-spikes of pale yellow fairly glow in the vapors and its hooded upper petal, acting as an umbrella, effectually keeps dry the stamens with their pollen nestling beneath it. Perfectly adapted to the special condition of its chosen habitat it laughs at danger and courts the overhanging precipice of the chasm. Coy, charming, alluring is this bewitching Child of the Mist. To see and caress her was the real object of my visit and her smile I found sufficient prize.

Early visitors to the Falls passed by this Child of the Mist without comment but the Engineer of the Zambesi Bridge, Mr. Francis Fox, found her, fell in love with her and dispatched her to grace his home garden in England. Later C. E. F. Allen, forester to the Rhodesian Railways, sent her to Kew where she blossomed freely and had her portrait placed in that Hall of Fame, the "Botanical Magazine." But she was really discovered in 1887, on the Usagara Mountains in rain-drenched Mozambique, by Mr. J. T. Last and sent to Kew Gardens where she first flowered and received her name in 1890. Though reared by Mother Nature under the peculiar climatic conditions of the Victoria Falls, this Gladiolus has proved as tractable under cultivation as she is beautiful. She has royally adapted herself and each season swells the number of her devoted admirers. If she is ever homesick no sign is apparent, yet at times she must think of the noise of thundering waters, of the glow of brilliant rainbows and of the perpetual cleansing bath her youth enjoyed in that Paradise, her home, the Victoria Falls of the Zambesi River.

PART II.

Australia

HOME OF BRILLIANT BLOSSOMS, OF GIANT
EUCALYPTS, OF FRAGRANT ACACIAS.

New Zealand

SCENIC ISLES MANTLED IN GREEN.

WESTERN AUSTRALIA

CHAPTER XIII.

A Fortunate Accident

IVE years after the discovery of America by Columbus in 1492, the Portuguese rounded the Cape of Good Hope and after 1498 their ships began to employ the Cape route to India and the East Indies. His Catholic Majesty, the King of Portugal, was a firm adherent of the Church of Rome which fanatically carried on its proselyting. On Portuguese ships men of other nations were often employed and not infrequently these men suffered at the hands of religious bigots and sought revenge when opportunity offered. This spirit appears to have infected Cornelis Houtman, a Dutchman, born at Gonda near Rotterdam, who had been in the employ of the Portuguese as an East India pilot and had suffered imprisonment at the hands of the Inquisition. In 1597, Houtman offered to lead an expedition of his own countrymen to the Indies. His offer was accepted, and resulted in the formation of the famous Dutch East India Company and the establishment of Dutch factories for trading purposes in Java and other Islands.

Prior to 1611, the customary course of ships after rounding the Cape of Good Hope was north to Madagascar and then directly east to Java. But it was discovered that by sailing about 3000 miles due east from the Cape, ships met with favorable winds and could then run north to Java and complete the voyage in several months less time. This change of route accidentally led to the discovery of Western Australia by the Dutch. In 1616, Dirk Hartog in the ship "Eendragt" landed at about latitude 26° 30' south, near the entrance to what is now called Shark Bay. Possibly, earlier voyagers had sighted the northwestern coast but Hartog seems to have been the first to land. The southwestern cape was discovered in 1622 by the ship "Leeuwin" ("Lioness") and bears her name to this day. The south coast was discovered by Pietre Nuyts, in 1627, who is fittingly commemorated by the genus Nuytsia, to which belongs the wonderful Christmas-tree of Western Australia. By 1665, the whole coast from the Gulf of Carpentaria south to the Leeuwin had been crudely mapped by the Dutch and the land named New Holland. Later, the name had wider application but the modern Western Australia is strictly the original New Holland.

The first Englishman to visit this newly discovered land was William Dampier, in 1688, on board the buccaneering ship "Swan" which put into what is now Cygnet Bay in the northwest for repairs. He paid a second visit in 1699 in command of the "Roebuck" and sailed along and examined the western and northwestern coasts. Dampier made the first collection of plants on the Australian continent and these (some forty in number) are preserved in the Herbarium of Oxford University. He is commemorated by Dampiera, a genus of dwarf, suffruticose plants remarkable for their intense blue flowers, and by the wonderful Desert Pea (*Clianthus Dampieri*).

The early discoverers were not impressed with what they saw. Dampier writes: "If it were not for that sort of pleasure which results from the discovery even of the barrenest spot upon the globe this coast of New Holland would not have charmed me much." It must be remembered that Dampier and the Dutch saw Australia from the sea and immediate vicinity where it looks forbidding, and no attempt to ascertain the real nature of the country and its possibilities were made for nearly two centuries after its whereabouts had become definitely known.

In 1696, a convoy of Dutch ships under Commander Willem de Vlaming and bound for Batavia, anchored off the island of Rottnest which was explored the next day and named for the abundance of rats' (Wallabies) nests found there. A few days later a landing was made on the mainland near the mouth of a river and the country explored for some forty miles inland. Black Swans were discovered on the river. Vlaming captured several and three were taken alive to Batavia. The river he named Black Swan River and on its banks today stands the flourishing capital city of Perth, but Vlaming reported that he had found neither good country nor seen anything worthy of note. When contrasted with the wealth of the East Indies and their luxuriant tropical vegetation, doubtless New Holland looked a barren, uninviting land.

The last quarter of the Eighteenth and the dawn of the Nineteenth Century saw increased activity in the exploration of the southern continent and with the energetic and enthusiastic Sir Joseph Banks, but lately returned from his voyage around the world with Captain Cook, a power in the land, no expedition sailed without the interests of botany and horticulture being properly taken care of. Indeed, Banks' energy inaugurated a veritable Golden Age in botanical discovery and plant introduction. Vancouver on his voyage to northwest America sighted Cape Leeuwin in 1791, and sailing eastward along the southern shore discovered and named King George's Sound, on the shores of which today stands the thriving town of Albany, and anchored there. With Vancouver was Archibald Menzies, surgeon and zealous naturalist, and a collection of plants made by Menzies was the first garnered in the rich region of southwest Australia. *Banksia Menziesii*, named for him by Robert Brown, commemorates the first botanist to land in Western Australia. In 1792, a French Expedition of discovery, under Admiral D'Entrecasteaux, visited New Holland with the naturalist J. J. Labillardière.

In 1801, Captain Flinders, who gave the name Australia to the southern continent, in the ship "Investigator" put into King George's Sound. With him were Robert Brown, the famous botanist, Ferdinand Bauer, botanical draughtsman, and Peter Good, a gardener from Kew, who assisted in the manual operations of collecting and preserving the plants. The "Investigator" was provided with a plant-cabin and the instructions to Captain Flinders were "to place the plant-cabin with the boxes of earth contained in it under the charge and care of the naturalist and gardener and to cause to be planted therein during the survey such plants, trees, shrubs etc., as they may think suitable for the Royal Gardens at Kew."

The botanical results obtained by this well-found expedition were incomparably greater than those of all previous voyages of a similar nature put together. At King George's Sound some 500 species were collected. Later large collections were made in other parts of Australia and safely landed in England. Flindersia, a genus of magnificent timber trees confined to northern New South Wales and Queensland, fittingly commemorates the famous navigator. The monotypic and endemic family, Brunoniaceae, composed of one species of herbs or dwarf suffruticose plants with bright blue flowers, is named for Brown. The east Australian genus Bauera, which are shrubs with twiggy, interlacing branches and rose-purple flowers, is named for Bauer. In our greenhouses *Bauera rubioides* is occasionally seen. Goodia, a genus of the Pea family, commemorates the gardener, Good.

It remains to mention another French Expedition —that commanded by Nicholas Baudin—which had on board the naturalist Leschenault and, anchoring off the mouth of the Black Swan River in 1802, explored it to the point where the city of Perth now stands. The naturalist above mentioned is immortalized in the genus Leschenaultia, a group of social plants whose flowers of every color are in Spring one of the sights of Western Australia. Baudin had also three gardeners on board and his expedition introduced many plants to France including the pretty *Kennedya coccinea.*

In 1825, strongly suspecting that France was about to found a settlement in Australia, the Governor of New South Wales sent a detachment of soldiers and a party of convicts to found a settlement at King George's Sound. In 1829, the British Flag was hoisted on the north side of the Swan River at its mouth by Captain Fremantle, who took formal possession in the name of King George IV of "all that part of New Holland which is not included within the territory of New South Wales." Thus Western Australia, a vast region some 1500 miles from north to south and 1000 miles from west to east with an area of some 975,920 square miles—more than six times the area of California and nearly one-third the size of the United States—became an integral part of the British Empire. By 1831, some 4000 persons were settled on Swan River with Perth as a centre and a fair start at colonization was made.

CHAPTER XIV.

Land of Prehistoric Plants

AVING dealt at some length with the discovery of Western Australia let us now devote a little time picturing to ourselves what sort of a land it really is and what its dominant arboreal and floristic characters are. It is true that physical features form the landscape of a country, especially when viewed from a distance; yet if its mountains, valleys and plains be the dominant notes it is to the character of its vegetative mantle that a country owes most for whatever esthetic charm it may possess. To a visitor from the Northern Hemisphere, no matter how familiar he or she may be with the forest scenery of the North. Western Australia is a new world. Nay, it might well be part of another planet so utterly different is the whole aspect of its vegetation. Intimate knowledge of the plants of the boreal regions only serves to accentuate the variance. In the North our trees in general have spreading umbrageous crowns, dark, often lustrous green leaves which set at right angles on the branches, cast a heavy shadow where man and beast alike may find cool shade from the noon-day heat in summer. In Western Australia the dominant trees have open, tufted crowns, gray or glaucous green leaves which hang vertically from the branches and cast little or no shadow. This difference in the color of the tree-foliage and the fact that the leaves are pendent instead of spreading on the branches may seem to the reader trivial matters, but in reality they completely change the aspect of the forests and profoundly influence the whole landscape as those familiar with the groves of Eucalyptus in California or South Africa will appreciate.

Western Australia is geologically the oldest part of Australia and is the original home of the typical Australian flora. Nearly the whole of the country is a vast plateau elevated from 1000 to 1500 feet above the sea, and planed down by erosive action of the elements. The western edge of this vast peneplain is fringed with coastal lowlands of Tertiary age. Some twenty miles east from Perth is the Darling scarp, produced by the faulting of the coastal strip and rising to some 1800 feet above sea-level. The central part of Australia was probably sea in Mesozoic times for what is now Australia was severed in Cretaceous times from north to south, but the west has not been submerged nor suffered much disturbance since the Middle-Palaeozoic age. The rocks are

Pre-Cambrian, largely crystalline schists and gneiss intersected with granites, diorites and serpentine. Much of the Darling scarp is capped with iron-stone laterite and to this the splendid Jarrah-tree (*Eucalyptus marginata*) is almost exclusively confined.

Near the coast in the south-west, limestone occurs and to this the Tuart (*Eucalyptus gomphocephala*) and other trees are peculiar. The diorites crop out as black or chocolate-colored patches and when disintegrated form wonderfully rich agricultural soils. The granites, weathered and disintegrated into fine white sand-like soil, form the so-called sand-plains where grow the wealth of plants which give Western Australia its chief floristic charm. The other rocks weather into fairly uniform red-brown earth.

I traversed Western Australia from west to east by the transcontinental railway but it was in the southwestern corner and on the goldfield areas round Kalgoorlie that my investigations were carried out. It is this southwest area that is so phenomenally rich in plants and we may well confine our attention to it.

In southwest Western Australia the rainfall is a winter one, from May to October, when from eighty to ninety per cent. of the annual total is precipitated. The summer (November to April) is dry except on the gold-fields. In the neighborhood of Perth the annual rainfall is about thirty-four inches. At Kalgoorlie it is about eight inches and further east virtually no rain falls in a year. Near the Leeuwin, where Karri (*Eucalyptus diversicolor*) grows, the annual rainfall is as much as forty inches. At Perth the mean annual temperature is 64°F., the maximum is 108°F. and the minimum 34°F. but these extremes are rarely reached.

The forests in general are referred to by the settlers as scrub—a derogatory term which they are far from meriting. They are open, often park-like, in character and the species of trees grow gregariously, but in the southwest corner there is a thick undergrowth of green-leafed bushes, chiefly Blue-bush (*Hovea Celsii* and other species) Hazel (*Chorilaena hirsuta* and *Trymalium Billardei*), and Water-bush (*Bossiaea aquifolium*). Vigorous lianas are unknown and what few climbing plants there are (Hardenbergias, Kennedyas, Clematis) have slender stems and are small. Where the rainfall is less than twelve inches a true scrub of stunted trees and shrubs is formed. As the rainfall becomes less and less so this scrub becomes more and more open but nowhere in the vicinity of the transcontinental line is there real desert although water may be unknown for possibly a hundred miles. Spiney Acacias, dull green Sage- and Salt-bush, and

Spinifex, especially adapted to dry conditions, grow in the most arid places. After a shower of rain innumerable herbs and suffruticose plants, such as Helipterum and Helichrysum—Everlastings with pink, white and yellow flowers; *Velleia rosea;* purple and pink Ptilotus; and many species of Goodenia, spring up, blossom and carpet the ground with color. Here and there a Kurrajong-tree (*Brachychiton Gregoryi*) with gouty trunks and scarlet flowers arrests attention. In the swollen trunk water is stored and the roots, which are succulent, are sometimes eaten by the aborigines.

The scrub is called "Mallee scrub" when dwarf Eucalypts predominate and "Mulga" when spiney Acacias and other prickly plants with small leaves and twiggy branches are in the ascendant. Flat or slightly rolling country covered with low scrub where there is little or nothing to break the monotony of open landscape is termed "Pindan." Large tracts are covered with harsh, greyish grasses known as "Spinifex," (*Triodia pungens, T. irritans* and others), some with viscid, others with non-sticky leaves. They grow thickly together in hummocky masses which prick the legs in an abominable manner if one attempts to pass through them. "Porcupine grasses" is another name applied to these pestiferous plants.

The Mulga scrub deserves a word or two. It is characterized by a thick to open growth of bushes of a uniform height of from 2 to 10 feet. The plants are twiggy and of dense habit with small leaves, all more or less prickly. In its typical form such Acacias as the Mulga (*A. aneura*) and Myall (*A. pendula*) dominate this scrub, but out of season so great is the similarity of growth that everything looks alike and deadly monotony is the outstanding feature. In spring and early summer all is changed. Diversity and not uniformity is then seen to characterize this scrub. Acacias, in which flattened branchlets carry out the functions of the leaves which are absent, abound and many of them are charming species when in full flower. The flowers are, of course, yellow, borne in little ball-like heads or on short spikes and are frequently delightfully fragrant. Some are merely prickly, others abominably spiney, and if one gets entangled among them the full meaning of Wait-a-while, Dead Finish, and other names or epithets applied by exasperated mining-prospectors and travelers to these unmannered shrubs is understood. Hakeas in seventy varieties, many with viciously spinescent branchlets, are prominent features and so too are Grevilleas, many of which have lovely blossoms. This is one of the largest of Australian genera and is very strongly developed in Western Australia where eighty-seven species occur, though the only one I know in cultivation here is G. *Thelemanniana*, a low shrub with pink and green flowers, very common round Perth.

Weird and extraordinary are the Grass-trees or Black-boys, *Kingia australis, Xanthorrhoea Preissii, X. reflexa* and other species, with curious mop-like heads of long, brittle, needle-shaped leaves. In the Kingia the flowers are borne on short drumstick-like affairs arranged in the form of a necklet; in the Xanthorrhoeas the inflorescence is a spear-like shaft thrust full six feet above the crown of leaves. Strange also is the Zamia Palm (*Macrozamia Fraseri*) with its short massive trunk, spreading crown of long, dark green, fern-like leaves, huge fruits with bright-colored seeds, poisonous in a raw state to cattle and man, as some of Vlaming's men were first to discover from unpleasant experience. This Zamia Palm is of very, very slow growth, a stem a yard high may be a hundred years or more old, yet strangely enough the fruit, which is oblong-ovoid, often 18 inches high and correspondingly thick and weighs fifty pounds and more, is developed in one season. These Grass-trees and Zamia Palms are trees of ancient lineage—relics of earlier geologic times—anachronisms.   In keeping with them are the Kangaroos, but the scene would be more complete if Rhinoceros and other pachydermatous animals were present or more in harmony still would be the presence of a Nothotherium, a Dinosaurus, a Plesiosaurus or some other monster of the remote Lizard Age.

CHAPTER XV.

Trees That Cast No Shadows

I N AUSTRALIA there are no Pines, Firs, Spruces nor Hemlocks, nor any other Conifer we of the North are familiar with. In Western Australia the family is represented by Callitris and Actinostrobus, two genera of small trees akin to Cupressus of the North. They are to be found on the coast, on the sand-plains and in the dry interior, growing more or less gregariously and up to middle age have twiggy branches and dense, bright to gray-green crowns. The wood is valuable, being very durable and in the ground well-nigh imperishable. Strongly resembling the Callitris, but in no way related, being in this respect nearer our Bayberry, are the Casuarinas, a group of numerous trees and shrubs with slender, whip-like, leafless branches and often pendent branchlets. They are depressing trees of sad aspect common by the sides of streams and as an under-storey in the Karri and other Eucalyptus forests. The bush species abound on the sand-plains and in the Mulga and Mallee scrub. The genus is typically Australian though one or two species are indigenous in the Malay Archi-pelago.

The dominant trees everywhere in Western Aus-tralia are, of course, the Eucalyptus, in fact, so much do they predominate that a casual observer might re-mark that there are no others.   In general these trees in Western Australia are of three types.   One, known as Gums, in which the trunks are smooth and polished, owing to the old bark being annually thrust off by the new; another, known as Stringybarks, in which the bark is fibrous and variously fissured. And the third, Bloodwoods, in which much resin is exuded and the bark often flakes off in patches. With their massive boles clad with striking barks, and their light, airy crowns the Eucalyptus make lovely photographic pictures but their gray-green, pendent foliage does not tend toward a refreshing landscape. This is all that need be said about them at the moment except that there is also a fourth group—the Mallees—which are confined to the interior and may be termed small trees or, better still, bushes. These Mallees have a much-thickened stool-like base from which shoots continue to grow for a number of years, then collapse and fall over and make way for their successors.

The classification of Eucalyptus in general has

proved a tremendous problem and is not yet fully solved, although the late Mr. J. H. Maiden, F.R.S., *facile princeps* among Australian botanists, steadily devoted more than three decades of a century to its solution. Yet the Western Australian species with few exceptions are clearly defined and easily recognizable.

The explanation in all probability is that in this ancient land of Western Australia, little or nothing has happened to seriously disturb the atmospheric equilibrium through aeons of time, and fixity of species has become established through this long sustained cycle of climatic stability. The inference is that the western species are older than their eastern kindred but it must not for one moment be supposed that they are in any way inferior in their morphological complexity. On the contrary, their development is perfect and of the highest order. The quality of their timber is second to none and of flowers they boast the largest and handsomest of the genus.

California and other parts of the world enjoying a similar climate are indebted to Western Australia for the red-flowered *Eucalyptus ficifolia*, truly a jewel beyond price among lesser trees. Had Western Australia given no other treasure to the world than this exquisite gem it would be entitled to a warm place in the affection of all flower-lovers. It may be news to many to learn that *E. ficifolia,* though widely planted in Australia itself and in other parts of the world, should as a wild tree be limited to a comparatively few acres between the Bow and Frankland Rivers in the southwest corner of Western Australia. I visited this district on purpose to see this tree and found it never above 40 feet in height with a short trunk, sometimes 10 feet in girth and a spreading crown occasionally 45 feet through. December is the month of its greatest floral display. The flowers vary in color from scarlet to orange-red, occasionally they are pink and sometimes white. The seeds are winged and this is the best character to distinguish the species from the closely related Marri (*E. calophylla*), a huge tree, abundant round Perth, with big urn-shaped fruits and large flowers, usually white but sometimes pink. In central Africa I have seen this species grown under the mistaken idea that it was *E. ficifolia,* and I have reason to believe that a similar confusion obtains in India and elsewhere.

Another lovely Eucalyptus is *E. torquata,* common near the goldfields, where less than a ten-inch rainfall occurs. This is a low, round-topped tree with thin branches and corymbose masses of orange to pink flowers but slightly inferior in size to those of the red-flowered species. I saw it in full bloom toward the end of November and thought what a lovely addition it would be to the gardens of Pasadena and elsewhere in the warm parts of this country.

Some of the bush or small tree forms (Mallees) like *E. tetraptera, E. pyriformis, E. erythrocorys, E. erythronema, E. Preissiana* and others have large pink, red or yellow flowers and are highly ornamental. This list could be extended fifty-fold but I will close with the inclusion of *E. macrocarpa*. In some ways this is the most extraordinary of all Eucalyptus. It is a straggly bush from 12 to 15 feet high and of no particular shape, with stout branches and never has other than the glaucous, opposite, decussate, sessile leaves characteristic of the juvenile stage of all Eucalyptus, but persistent through the life of the plant in very few species. The flowers are axillary, 5 to 6 inches across, and of a brilliant orange hue. To me this Eucalyptus was a plant to marvel at and I sincerely hope it will thrive in Pasadena where I was instrumental in sending seeds together with those of *E. torquata* and the Mallees named above.

In swampy ground and by sides of streams grow species of Melaleuca of which *M. rhaphiophylla, M.*

parviflora and *M. striata* are the most common. They are not tall trees but they often have thick trunks which are clothed with thin, papery bark partially exfoliated and remaining in shaggy masses as in our River Birch.   Paper-barks is their vernacular name. By river-sides, in swamps, on sand-plains and in the open, park-like Eucalyptus forests grow different species of Banksia with greenish white, yellow and red flowers.   These are among the most wonderful flowering trees of Australia, yet very few are in cultivation in this country and, so far as I can discover, only one (*B. prionites*) of the thirty-seven known Western Australian species.   All have striking leaves, more or less deeply sinuous along the margins, and erect cone-like heads of flowers, rich in honey. The most remarkable is *B. grandis* which is common in the Jarrah forests as a low, stoutly branched tree with 8-inch cones of yellow flowers.   The tallest is *B. verticillata,* the River Banksia, which is often 60 feet tall and yields valuable timber.   By-the-way, all the Banksias and indeed their family (Proteacea) generally have beautifully figured wood highly suitable for cabinet work, inlaying and veneering. *Banksia Menziesii, B. attenuata, B. littoralis, B. ilicifolia* are all striking plants which California ought to possess, but I must reserve a special word of praise for the lovely *B. coccinea*, a bush, common round Albany, with rounded heads of crimson flowers.

Acacias in variety as small trees are common in all sorts of situations but none of these Western Australian sorts are much known in America; *Acacia cyanophylla*, *A. cyclops* and *A. saligna* are common species. All the Acacias are worthy plants and shall be more fully dealt with in a subsequent chapter. I may say now that on the sand-plains the charming *A. pulchella*, *A. Drummondii* and the well-known *A. armata* are abundant and in no account of the Western Australia flora should reference to *A. acuminata*, the Umbrella Bush or Raspberry Jam Tree, be omitted. This is a low, round-topped social tree with twiggy branches and narrow, light green phyllodes in lieu of leaves and short axillary spikes of clear yellow flowers. It is a feature of the wheatbelt where it forms open woods and its presence denotes good land. Its timber, which has exactly the odor of raspberry jam, lasts a life-time in the ground and is highly appreciated by the farmer for fencing posts, so it is safe from actual extermination even on good agricultural land.

As an under-storey in the Tuart (*Eucalyptus gomphocephala*) forests grows *Agonis flexuosa*, known as Peppermint—a charming tree with slender,

pendent branches suggesting a Weeping Willow and
in season studded with pure white flowers which arise
from every leaf-axil. For California and the warm
South this tree would be most valuable. I do not find
it mentioned in Bailey's "Cyclopedia." An ugly tree
but with handsomely figured wood is *Xylomelum oc-
cidentale* with an inedible pear-like fruit from which
the name Wooden Pear is derived. Hakeas (Needle-
bushes) in variety with axillary clusters of flowers
and often with narrow spiney foliage, are common
as small trees. Among them are *Hakea suaveolens,
H. elliptica* (both with white flowers and the latter
with relatively broad leaves) and *H. laurina* with
crimson flowers and known on the Riviera as the
"Glory of the Garden." These three are in cultivation in California, I believe, and they would make
valuable hedge-plants in the hot and drier parts of
this country. The Agonis and various Leptosper-
mums would also make good hedge-plants in southern California.

A remarkable tree of the sand-plains is *Nuytsia
floribunda* which is parasitic on the roots of many
plants and is first cousin to our Mistletoe. Imagine
a gigantic mass of Mistletoe in the form of a tree 30
feet or more tall and as much in diameter, a trunk 5
feet in girth, and leaves little in evidence on the

rounded green shoots, and you have the Nuytsia as it appears for the greater part of the year. In December it bursts into bloom, huge panicles of brilliant orange-colored flowers terminating every branch. Locally known as the Christmas-tree, it is in blossom one of the gorgeous floral sights of the world. Being a semi-parasite it cannot be cultivated in our gardens but it is worth a journey to Western Australia to see this feast of wonderful color.

Two other parasitic trees must be noted. One (*Fusanus acuminatus*) yields a round, orange-red edible fruit and is known as the Quandong or Australian Peach. The other (*Santalum cygnorum*) is a Sandal-wood of great economic importance, the wood being exported in quantity to China where it is used as incense. The streets of Hongkong, Canton and other cities reek with its powerful but pleasant odor.

CHAPTER XVI.

Fairyland of Flowers

RILLIANT inflorescences are characteristic of the Western Australia flora but they attain their greatest exuberance on the so-called "Sand-plains." These are really vast gardens where numberless species riot in color. A remarkable feature of these sand-plains is the extraordinary number of twiggy suffruticose plants, usually tufted in habit with large, woody rootstocks and from 9 to 18 inches high. They are all strange to us of the North, but in color the blues of Dampiera and certain Leschenaultias outdo our Gentians just as Platytheca, Tetratheca and Boronia outvie our Hardy Heaths and rival the glorious Ericas of the Cape of Good Hope. In yellow the Hibbertias and Condolleas excel our shrubby Cinquefoils and dispute with our Hypericums and Buttercups. But enough—comparisons are rightly termed odious. Each country possesses floristic gems and gardens claim the best from all lands.

Of the plants of the Western Australian sand-plains in our gardens today *Boronia megastigma* with fragrant, maroon-purple flowers, greenish yellow within, *B. elatior* with dark red-brown to rose-red, and *B. heterophylla* with scarlet to crimson flowers are perhaps the most widely known. These are partial to swampy places and are diffuse shrubs from 3 to 10 feet tall with twiggy branches bearing flowers in the leaf-axils. There are thirty-four other species in Western Australia, some with pink flowers. Next we may place *Pimelea spectabilis* with pink to white, *P. rosea* with pink and *P. suaveolens* with yellowish to rose-colored flowers. These relatives of our Daphnes are twiggy shrubs of neat, compact habit and flowers clustered in terminal heads. These are three out of the twenty-eight species indigenous in Western Australia.

Of the eleven species of Tetratheca only *T. hirsuta* is in our gardens. This is a genus of beautiful and floriferous shrubs with twiggy branches, small leaves and pink blossoms. Of the related Platytheca, another Heath-like plant with purple flowers, there is but one species known (*P. galioides*) and this is in our possession. Dampiera is apparently unknown to America gardens but the fourteen species of the related Leschenaultia are represented by *L. formosa* with orange and scarlet, *L. grandiflora* with orange and purple-red, *L. laricina* with white, lilac and red, and *L. biloba* with dark blue flowers. These are

Heath-like, often social plants remarkable for their richly colored blossoms. Communities of Dampiera and Leschenaultia with myriad flowers of the most exquisite shades of blue, orange and scarlet, once seen can never be forgotten.

Chorizemas with small, lustrous green, Holly-like leaves and orange to scarlet or purple-red flowers in racemes are peculiarly Western Australian. Three species, *C. varium, C. cordatum* and *C. ilicifolium,* are grown here out of the fourteen species known. The curious *Darwinia Hookeriana* and *D. macrostegia* are sometimes seen in the gardens and so, too, is the wonderful Glory Pea (*Clianthus Dampieri*) with its gray, hairy leaves and intense scarlet, blotched with black flowers. The latter is native of the arid regions of the interior and has proved extraordinarily difficult to cultivate. By crown-grafting seedlings on the cotyledonary stage of the Bladder-senna (*Colutea arborescens*)—a delicate operation—the Glory Pea may be successfully grown if great care be exercised in watering the plants.

A suffruticose member of the Parsley family, *Actinotus rotundifolius,* with white fading to pink, bracteate flowers arranged in flattened umbels in the form of a cross and known as the Southern Cross, is worthy of note though I am afraid lost to our gardens.

Of the forty-six species of Hibbertia only one (*H. perfoliata*) is in our gardens and Templetonia, with six, is represented ·by *T. retusa*. The curious Dryandra, akin to Banksia, with forty-seven species is unknown here and so, too, are such pleasing and floriferous shrubs as Bossiaea with sixteen species, Thomasia—twenty-five species, Dodonaea—twenty-two species, Goodenia—thirty-eight species, Leucopogon—100 species, Verticordia—forty species, and Eremophila with fifty-one species. In dainty elegance *Verticordia oculata* is a princess among Australia's small shrubs and Eremophila, known as Desert-pride, is aptly named for it glorifies the most arid regions and, mixed with stretches of Everlastings, forms vast natural gardens, the splendor and grace of which no art can hope to successfully imitate.

Suggestive of a heavy snow-fall just thawing so as to show a little of the herbage are the Smoke-bushes (*Conospermum floribundum* and *C. staechadis*). These remarkable shrubs are often gregarious and have such copious tomentose, white or gray inflorescences as to give the appearance of smoking bushes.

Trees are rare on the sand-plains but among the

shrubs growing from 4 to 10 feet high are many species of Eriostemon, Crowea, Grevillea, Baeckia, Casuarina, Persoonia, Acacia, Lachnostachys, Isopogon, Lambertia, Beaufortia, Leptospermum and Melaleuca (called Tea-trees), Calycothrix (Fringed Myrtles), *Callistemon speciosus* and *C. phoeniceus* known as Bottle-brushes. I will close the list with mention of the lovely Geraldton Wax-flower (*Chamaelaucium uncinatum*) unknown, I fear, to American gardens. This is a large bush with slender branches, pink, saucer-shape, waxy flowers, long-persistent on the branches and produced in great profusion. Its beauty has won for it a peculiar place in the affections of Australians and it ought to be grown in California and, indeed, in every land where a suitable climate obtains.

Climbing plants are almost negligible in Western Australia being represented by slender, twining plants like Sollya, Clematis and Hardenbergia, the pretty *Kennedya coccinea* and the vigorous *K. nigricans,* both well-known in California.

Western Australia is pre-eminently a land of woody plants, and herbs are comparatively few in genera and species. But what they lack in this respect they make up in numbers. On the sand-plains and the open scrub of the arid regions they carpet the

ground.   Where rain falls but infrequently they
spring up in myriads almost over-night and burst
into sheets of bloom.   It is difficult to draw a line
between suffruticose plants and true herbs and many,
like Stylidium, for example, may be justly classed
with either.   These Stylidiums, represented by sixty-
four species, are called Trigger-plants.   The stamen-
filaments are connate around the style which is curved
and when touched by an insect suddenly straightens
itself with a jerk and scatters the pollen.   They are
tufted plants with erect, foot-high racemes of small
white, pink, yellow and orange-colored flowers.
Some six species are in cultivation.

In the North our meadows, swamps, glades and
margins of woods owe much of their floral beauty
to such Compositae as Goldenrods, Asters and
Daisies in variety, and this family with its gregarious
Everlastings beautifies vast areas of Western Australia with glistening, paleaceous florets.   Most if
not all of these Everlastings are annuals, and include
many species of Helipterum, Helichrysum, Podole-
pis, Angianthus and Waitzia.   Of the thirty-one
species of Helipterum the best known is the dainty
H. Manglesii often called Rhodanthe; *H. roseum* has
large solitary flowers and *H. Humboldtianum* yellow
flowers in dense terminal corymbs.   *Helichrysum api-*

culatum has small yellow flowers; *Waitzia grandi-flora* and *W. aurea*, the only species we grow out of the twenty-eight known, have yellow heads, each 2 inches across, collected into large corymbs. The Swan River Daisy (*Brachycome iberidifolia*), an annual growing from 6 to 18 inches tall with leaves divided into narrow segments and flowers blue, rose or white, is familiar to us and is one of eleven species known. The endemic and monotypic *Brunonia australis* with its pretty blue heads of flowers terminating each stem suggests some little Scabious of European meadows. This is a variable plant and fittingly is found all over Australia.

No Iris grows in Australasia but the genus Patersonia takes the place and of the fourteen Western Australian species *P. occidentalis*, with sapphire-blue flowers, is known to our gardens from the neighborhood of Perth. Very common are the curious Anigozanthos, known in the vernacular as Kangaroo-paws. These odd-looking plants, distant relatives of Ophiopogon and Sanseviera, have sedge-like leaves, flowers of brilliant bizarre colors arranged on a one-sided raceme terminating a scape from 1 to 2 feet tall; in *A. pulcherrima* the raceme is branched. The perianth-tube is much elongated and has short, flattened, expanded lobes resembling the paw of a Kangaroo in miniature. The flowers are woolly, red, yellow, green, purple to purple-brown and on each there is usually a combination of two or more of these colors. Of the nine species, *A. flavida*, *A. Manglesii* and *A. pulcherrima* are occasionally seen in our gardens.

The pretty Fringed Violet (Thysanotis) boasts fourteen species, of which two (*T. dichotomus* and *T. multiflorus*) are in cultivation. These are small plants with grass-like leaves and flowers of violet color, fringed at the edges. Of Sundews (Drosera) thirty-one species are recognized in Western Australia and one (*D. gigantea*) grows 3 feet tall. The related *Byblis gigantea* grows from 1 to 2 feet tall, has 10 to 12 inch long filiform leaves and purple flowers each 1½ inches across. In peat swamps round Albany, sheltering beneath tussocks of coarse herbage and very difficult to find, grows *Cephalotus follicularis*, the Western Australian Pitcher-plant, in which the radical leaves are converted into tiny pitchers that trap small insects.

Many ground Orchids, some with striking flowers, grow in Western Australia but there are no epiphytic species. Succulent plants, so important a feature in South Africa, Mexico, and some of the dry southwestern States of this country, are rare in Western Australia, although two species of Mesembryanthemum (*M. aequilaterale* and *M. australe*) are wide-spread and abundant but I doubt if they be genuine members of the Australian flora. Ferns, save a few species which can withstand dessication, are almost non-existent. No Tree-fern is known in Western Australia but in many parts the common Bracken abounds.

Upwards of 4000 species of plants are known to be indigenous in Western Australia; four-fifths of them are peculiar to the country and not found even in Eastern Australia. Alas! scarcely forty of these are known to American gardens, yet at least half of them would flourish in California and the warmer States. Since this work is for the appetite of garden-lovers especially no purpose would be served in mentioning plants whose surnames even are unknown in the gardens of the North. I content myself with lifting the tiniest corner of the veil to tell of an odd plant here and there whose name is known though often vaguely. Colored pictures of many Western Australian or New Holland plants may be found in the "Botanical Magazine," "Botanical Register," and other periodicals published in the thirties and forties of last century but lack of sun caused many to disappear from cultivation in Europe very early and one regrets that in those days there were no Californian gardens to receive them into safety. Had such existed my story would have been of familiar and not unfamiliar plants.

EASTERN AUSTRALIA

CHAPTER XVII.

Botany Bay

 TABLET fixed on a rock at Botany Bay in 1821, records the discovery of Eastern Australia in the following words: "A. D. MDCCLXX. Under the auspices of British science, these shores were discovered by James Cook and Joseph Banks, the Columbus and Maecenas of their time." The northern shores of Australia appear to have been first discovered by a Portuguese, Manoel Heredia (or Eredia) in 1601. In 1605, the Dutch yacht "Duyfhen" sailed down the Gulf of Carpentaria as far as Cape Keer Weer (Turn again) but thought the land was part of New Guinea. A Spaniard, Luis de Torres, in 1606, discovered the neck of the water which separates the extreme northern tip of Australia from New Guinea and now called Torres Strait. The famous Dutch navigator, Abel Tasman, in 1642 discovered what is now known as Tasmania and, unaware that it was an island, named it Van Dieman's Land, after the Governor of Batavia under whose command the exploration work was done. But no one appears to have seen the eastern shores of the austral continent until the coming of Captain Cook in 1770. The particular object of Cook's first voyage, as is well-known, was to observe the transit of the planet Venus, but why Tahiti in the Society Islands was selected for the place and the subsequent events which lead to momentous results are worth recording here.

In February, 1768, the Council of the Royal Society addressed a memorial to King George III, the first paragraph of which reads: . . . . "That the passage of the Planet Venus over the disc of the sun which will happen on the 3rd of June, in the year 1769, is a phenomenon that must, if the same be accurately observed in proper places, contribute greatly to the improvement of astronomy on which navigation so much depends." Later on it states . . . . "The like appearance will not happen for more than one hundred years." The Royal Society indicated as suitable any place not exceeding 30 degrees of southern latitude, and between the 140th and 180th degrees of longtitude west from Greenwich."

It is on record that California was thought of as an observing station. Early in 1768 the British Ambassador at Madrid applied to the Court of Spain for the "grant of a passport to a ship designed for California, to observe the Transit of Venus." This was promised with the proviso that the astronomer should be a member of the Roman Catholic Church. An Italian gentleman was consequently engaged for the undertaking, but the passport when demanded was refused by the Spanish Ministry, who alleged that it was repugnant to the policy of the government to admit foreigners into their American ports unless driven there by necessity, and especially those who by their profession would be fitted to make such observations as might facilitate the approaches and descents of their enemies at any future war.

It is curious how affairs work out. I have shown how persecution by the Inquisition led indirectly to the formation of the Dutch East India Company, and, fortuitously, to the discovery of Western Australia. Now this refusal of the Spanish Ministry to grant a passport for a ship to visit California also resulted indirectly, of course, in the discovery of Eastern Australia. The British Government acquired a vessel of 368 tons, named her the "Endeavor" and placed Captain James Cook in command. Tahiti was selected as the place for observation and the vessel sailed from Plymouth on August 25, 1768. Mr. Charles Green was the astronomer appointed, and, at his own expense, Joseph Banks, his assistant

Dr. Carl Solander, with attendants (eight in number) and a full equipment, accompanied Captain Cook. The orders of the Lords of the Admiralty were that after the observations on the Transit of Venus were finished the "Endeavor" was to "proceed under the direction of Mr. Banks on further discoveries of the great Southern Continent."

The voyage was made by rounding Cape Horn, and Tahiti was reached on April 13, 1769. The Transit of Venus was successfully observed on the fated 3rd of June under perfect atmospheric conditions and on July 13th the "Endeavor" sailed for New Zealand, arriving there on October 8th. Then began the circumnavigation of New Zealand, which was accomplished by February 26, 1770. Casting round for "new worlds to conquer" it was decided to "stand immediately to the westward, fall in with the coast of New Holland as soon as possible and then sail to the northward." This resulted in the discovery of New South Wales and "another continent was added to the world."

The "Endeavor" sailed from Admiralty Bay (Cape Farewell) in New Zealand on March 31st; the Australian coast was sighted on April 19th; and a landing made on April 28th, the place being named Botany Bay from the wealth of new and strange plants found there. After a week's stay the voyage was continued coastwise and northward, Moreton Bay, Bustard Bay, Endeavour River were discovered and named, together with other places, and Cook "took possession of the whole eastern coast by the name of New South Wales." On the 27th of August, Australia was left and the course laid for New Guinea. This is not the place to pursue further the interesting story of early voyagers to Australia but one thing more is perhaps worthy of record here. In 1783, James Matra, who had been a midshipman with Cook, submitted to the Government a scheme for establishing in New South Wales a colony wherein Great Britain might afford an asylum to the American loyalists who had been rendered homeless by the result of the War of Independence and where they might "repair their broken fortunes and again enjoy their former domestic felicity." The loyalists found homes in Canada, and New South Wales unfortunately became a penal settlement.

The original New South Wales is an enormous tract of country about two-thirds the size of the United States of America. It is now divided into four states—Queensland, New South Wales, Victoria, and South Australia; with Brisbane, Sydney, Melbourne and Adelaide as their respective capitals.

In each of these cities are well-found Botanic Gardens whose influence I shall have occasion to speak of later. In Cretaceous times an aqueous barrier divided the continent from north to south and this, today, is represented by arid and in parts desert country. Much of Queensland is within the tropics and this I shall not deal with here. Tasmania is botanically a province of Victoria with certain features of its own. The arid regions of central Australia are in general similar to those of Western Australia with which they are contiguous and are omitted in consequence.

The boundaries between the states are purely political and artificial, and the whole of the country included in our review is largely a cordillera forming a fairly complete bulwark barring out the Pacific Ocean from the central plains. The highest peak of the system is Mount Kosciusko, with an altitude of 7346 feet above sea-level, which carries snow for many months of the year, indeed, in sheltered crevices the year round. There are other peaks over 7000 feet high and much of the southwest in particular is wild and mountainous.

In contradistinction to Western Australia the rainfall of Eastern Australia is largely a summer rainfall although over much of the territory it is fairly distributed throughout the year. South Australia is the dryest of the eastern states and in Adelaide the annual rainfall averages twenty-four inches, which is less than that of any other of the Australian capital cities. Over the coastal areas the rainfall is essentially a winter one. Tasmania has for its size a most remarkably varied climate and the annual rainfall varies from eighteen inches in the east to 145 inches (Mt. Read) on the west coast. At Hobart, the capital, the annual rainfall is a little over twenty-four inches. On the highlands of Tasmania snow falls throughout every month of the year though it does not lie except in the winter months. During the winter period snow falls on the mountain ranges of the southeastern part of Australia proper.

CHAPTER XVIII.

Treasures of the Brush

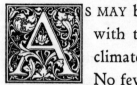S MAY be expected the eastern highlands with their varied range in altitude, in climate and soils support a rich flora. No fewer than 5000 species are known to grow there south of the tropic but the floristic features are much less striking than those of Western Australia. The coast belt and coastal tablelands of eastern Australia, well-watered and with rich soils, support rain-forests which are termed "brush." The term "scrub" is occasionally applied but the tendency is to relegate this term to the open, park-like forests of the dryer interior regions.

In the brush broad-leaf evergreen trees with umbrageous crowns and green leaves set at right angles on the branchlets and casting a heavy shade predominate over the familiar Eucalyptus. Lianas are common together with epiphytic plants and a dense, green undergrowth of shrubs. In other words, the vegetation of the rain-forests is luxuriant, but eastern Australia in general lacks the wealth of brilliant inflorescences characteristic of the sand-plains of Western Australia. On the highest mountains, and in Tasmania in particular, grow many alpine plants.

Curiously enough it is in western Tasmania that the rain-forests reach their maximum density. In these luxuriates the remarkable Horizontal Wood (*Anodopetalum biglandulosum*), a tree with horizontally spreading branches densely matted above one another, rendering the floor of the forest quite impassable.

In Eastern Australia the Eucalypts attain their maximum development both in height and taxonomic complexity, and yet in size of flower and brilliancy of color they fall behind and cannot compare with many of their Western Australian brethren. Individual trees of Ironbark (*E. sideroxylon*) are commonly seen with pink or crimson flowers but, though pretty these are small. In the others the flowers are white or cream-colored and no east Australian Eucalyptus even approximates in beauty to the red-flowered *E. ficifolia* of the western state, to mention no other. I may say that sepals and petals are absent in all Eucalypts and when the color of the flowers is mentioned it is that of the stamens that is really meant.

The tallest known Eucalypts grow in Gippsland, Victoria, and are referable to *E. regnans*. The height of these trees has been much exaggerated, as much as 525 feet having been stated. The tallest tree authentically measured was 375 feet, which leaves a good margin in its favor over the 340-foot Redwood (*Sequoia sempervirens*) measured as it lay on the ground by Professor Sargent near Scotia on the Eel River, California, in September, 1896.

Other giant Eucalypts are the Blackbutt (*E. pilularis*) and the Tallow-wood (*E. microcorys*). Indeed, many species grow to an enormous size, including *E. globulus* which is the Eucalypt best known to us of the North and in the minds of many does duty for the whole family. Of the seventy-six species enumerated in the "Standard Cyclopedia of Horticulture" as being in cultivation in this country sixty-six are native of Eastern Australia. The genus was founded on *E. obliqua* by L'Heritier on material collected by David Nelson at Adventure Bay, Tasmania, in January, 1777, though members of the genus were earlier seen and collected by Banks and Solander at Botany Bay and elsewhere. It was Banks at Bustard Bay in May, 1770, that first applied to them the name of Gumtrees, now universally adopted in Australia.

The Eucalypts are Australia's greatest gift to forestry. They are now planted in immense numbers in Africa and South America; to a less extent in California, New Zealand, southern India and the regions bordering the Mediterranean. As the work of afforestation proceeds Eucalypts will be more and more planted and where climate is suitable they are destined to be the favored ones above all other hard-wood trees. Their rapid growth and their wide range of useful timbers give them advantage over all other broad-leaf trees in the practice of commercial forestry.

The Waratah (*Telopea speciosissima*), which some would make the national flower of New South Wales, is a large bush or small tree with deeply toothed, coriaceous leaves, oblong with a narrowed base, and terminal, subglobose heads of from 3 to 4 inches through of crimson flowers rather suggesting a large Chrysanthemum. Related to Telopea is the Wheel-tree, of which three species (*Stenocarpus sinuatus, S. Cunninghamii* and *S. salignus*) are in cultivation. These are large trees, natives of the brush, with leaves clustered at the ends of the branches and flowers arranged in candelabrum-like umbels with each unopened flower radiating outward like the spokes of a wheel. The handsomest is *S. sinuatus* with flowers bright orange-red tipped with yellow. The inflorescence is clothed with attractive

144

orange-scarlet, silky hairs and when all the flowers of an umbel are open it suggests a Tacsonia flower.

Well-known to us of the North, being raised as an annual pot-plant by nurserymen for table decoration on account of its elegant much-divided foliage, is the Silky Oak (*Grevillea robusta*). This is one of the handsomest of Australian flowering trees and has richly figured wood valuable for furniture and cabinet-making. The flowers are orange-yellow borne erect on one-sided racemes freely produced along the branchlets. As in other Proteaceae the long-persistent fruits are a drawback, being rather unsightly. The Silky Oak is a fast growing tree, much planted in many parts of the world, either for its beauty or to produce the necessary shade over Coffee, Cocoa and other tropical crops. Another species (*G. Hilliana*) is also a large tree with foliage rather like that of *Stenocarpus sinuatus* and greenish white flowers borne on erect, axillary, cylindrical racemes each from 6 to 8 inches long. Among the shrubs are many other species of Grevillea, including *G. rosmarinifolia* with pink and *G. juniperina* with yellow flowers, which are fairly hardy in the south of England, and the red-flowered *G. Banksii* with fine divided foliage.

A number of Banksias, both trees and bushes, are striking features. Among them are *B. integrifolia*,

B. latifolia, B. serrata and the low-growing charming *B. ericifolia,* all with yellowish flowers and occasionally grown in California though this fine genus has hardly got a foothold in our gardens. Lastly, among the handsome Proteaceae, so glorious a feature of the Australian flora, I may mention the Queensland Nut (*Macadamia ternifolia*). This is a small tree, seldom exceeding 30 feet, with ternate leaves, long racemes of whitish flowers and nuts about 1 inch in diameter, edible, of excellent flavor, and very nutritious.

Very handsome in flower is the Black-Bean (*Castanospermum australe*) with racemes of fleshy, yellow to coral-red blossoms freely produced from the old branches; it has pinnate leaves a foot and a half long, and pods from 8 to 9 inches long and 2 inches broad, containing seeds which, though edible, are not wholesome.

The Melaleucas or Tea Trees are common, some species being tall trees and other bushes. The largest is *M. Leucodendron,* abundant near the coast, with relatively large white flowers and shaggy masses of buff-colored changing to white bark. Another tree species is *M. styphelioides* with smaller creamy white flowers in dense spikes, small prickly green leaves and spongy thick bark; *M. ericifolia* is a small tree and

M. armillaris a shrub with pendent branchlets. More showy are the Bottle-brushes (Callistemon) of which *C. lanceolatus, C. rigidus, C. brachyandrus* and *C. salignus* are grown in California.

The largest genus of plants in Australia is Acacia, of which some 415 species have been described and of these 280 are Eastern. Wattle, prefixed by such terms as Silver, Golden, Black, Green, etc., is the general name for them and their importance entitles them to a special chapter. Belonging to the same family as the Acacias but to another section is the Batswing Coral (*Erythrina vespertilio*). This tree is a gorgeous sight when in blossom with its scarlet flowers in masses on the leafless branches. The leaves are remarkable in form being oddly cuneate in shape and suggestive of a bat's wing, as its common name would lead one to suppose.

Different plants designated Christmas-trees or -bushes occur in several states and they are all handsome when in flower which happens around Christmas-time. In New South Wales it is *Ceratopetalum gummiferum,* a small tree with trifoliolate leaves and terminal cymose clusters of blooms. Each flower has notched petals and four persistent calyx-lobes which enlarge and become red-colored after the petals and stamens have fallen. Allied to this Christmas-tree is the lovely *Eucryphia Billardieri*, the Pink Wood of Tasmania, a bush or tree of moderate size with glistening resinous winter-buds, opposite leaves pale on the underside, and snow-white flowers each an inch across. There are other species of Eucryphia in Tasmania but outside of this island the genus is known only from South America.

Another link between Tasmania and South America, and this with species in Eastern Australia and New Zealand, is found in the genus Nothofagus of which there are several species. They are mainly trees with numerous, slender branchlets and small myrtle-like leaves. They often grow gregariously and from their manner of branching singularly resemble our Hemlock (*Tsuga canadensis*). One species (*Nothofagus Gunnii*) is deciduous and has the distinction of being the only deciduous tree in Tasmania. There are no Willows, Birches, Poplars, Alders, Elms, Walnuts nor Hickories in Australia and the great family to which belong our Oaks, Hazels, Chestnuts and Beeches, so all-important a feature of our northern forests, is represented solely by Nothofagus variously known as Myrtle, Birch and Southern Beech.

Two members of the large and widely dispersed Fig-family that must not be omitted in any sketch of the tree flora of Eastern Australia are *Ficus macrophylla* and *F. rubiginosa*. They are widely branching umbrageous trees with large trunks and surface-spreading roots. Both are excellent cattle-feed. The first-named is known as the Moreton Bay Fig, from the place of its discovery, and with its large leaves is reminiscent of the Rubber-tree of the florist; the other is indigenous round Sydney and has small, neat, lustrous leaves, and an umbrella-like crown, and is an excellent subject for planting where soil thinly covers hard rock. Both are fine avenue trees.

One of the oddities of the Australian tree-world is the genus Exocarpus, to which belongs the Native Cherry which has the "stone outside the fruit." The best known is *E. cupressiformis*, a leafless plant with bright green, slender branches densely arranged and in appearance suggestive of a Cypress. The "stone" is really the fruit which is seated on a red, fleshy receptacle. This tree is a root-parasite belonging to the Sandal-wood family and not very far removed from our Mistletoe. It is widely dispersed in the scrub of Eastern Australia.

South of the tropic Palms are poorly represented in Australia. In the rain-forests the Bangalow (*Archontophoenix Cunninghamiana*), with slender stems 30 to 50 feet tall and graceful crown of pinnate leaves, and the Fan-leaf Cabbage Palm (*Livistona australis*) are abundant. The Cabbage Palm is found well south into Victoria and is very handsome with its polished dark green leaves and petioles armed with brown hooks. Another species (*L. Mariae*) is the only Palm in central Australia and is confined to a very limited area on the Macdonnell Range. A Ratan (*Calamus Muelleri*) and a Walking-stick Palm (*Linospadix monostachyus*) grow also in the rain-forests; and indigenous on Lord Howe's Island are *Kentia Fosteriana* and *K. Belmoreana*, now indispensable to our florists, and also the lesser known *K. canterburyana*.

In Conifers Eastern Australia is much richer than the western part of the continent, yet, except Callitris in the drier interior regions, they are nowhere a dominant feature of the forests. There are quite a number of species of Callitris and inland, where the rainfall is sparse, wide tracts are covered with the white and black Cypress Pines (*C. robusta* and *C. calcarata*) respectively. On the coast grow *C. arenosa* and *C. rhomboidea;* of these the first-named is a handsome tree with a blackish green, billowy crown and a rugged trunk. The Queensland Kauri (*Agathis robusta*) just comes within our limits and is a noble tree with a column-like bole, clothed with scaly bark, a shapely crown and leathery dark green oblong, lance-shaped leaves. The remarkable Bunya-Bunya (*Araucaria Bidwillii*) is a close relative of the Monkey-Puzzle of gardeners (*A. imbricata*) which is native of Chili. The Bunya-Bunya up to middle age is a striking tree with a perfect dome-shaped crown, but afterwards it becomes scrawny and ugly. The cone, as large as a child's head, disintegrates and falls when ripe. Its large seed is good eating and is much sought after by the Blacks and by the Kangaroos. On the volcanic Norfolk Island, fringing the ocean and nowhere else, grows the familiar *Araucaria excelsa* and on the mainland the related *A. Cunninghamii* which has less regularly arranged branches and branchlets. The wood of these Araucarias and of the Kauri is very valuable timber and the trees are being rapidly felled.

None of our northern genera of Conifers grow wild in Australia and the great family Pinaceae is represented by the genus Athrotaxis of which there are three species all confined to Tasmania. Though not of large size they are important timber trees; two (*A. cupressoides* and *A. selaginoides*) are known as King William Pines and the third (*A. laxifolia*) as Red Pine from the color of its wood. No Yew is native of the austral continent but of the related genus

Podocarpus there are several species, locally known as "Damsons" from their fruits. There are several other related genera with one exception (*Pherosphaera Fitzgeraldii*) all confined to Tasmania. The best known are the Huon Pine (*Dacrydium Franklinii*) and the Celery-Top Pine (*Phyllocladus rhomboidalis*), both lovely trees scarcely known to our northern gardens.

The ancient family of Cycads is represented by three genera. Of Macrozamia sixteen species have been recognized but it is probable that some are merely variant forms. One of the best known is *M. spiralis*, widespread in New South Wales. Two larger growing species are *M. Perowskiana* and *M. Moorei* but the giant of the genus is *M. Hopei*, specimens of which are said to grow 60 feet tall. This species is doubtfully wild south of the tropic and the same is true of the curious *Bowenia spectabilis* and *B. serrulata*. Cycas itself is confined to the tropics in Australia. Apart from their great botanical interest these old aristocrats are all handsome garden plants.

CHAPTER XIX.

Pageantry of Shrub and Herb

THE drier regions reproduce many of the features of Western Australia; Mulga and Mallee scrub and Spinifex occur. Various species of Xanthorrhoea are scattered over the country and are a feature of some of the sandy islands immediately off the coast. Shrubs are plentiful and the variety is great though on the whole their blossoms are much less conspicuous and their garden value inferior to their congeners of Western Australia. Epacris is an exception and this is the genus best known to us among the east Australian shrubs though of the thirty known species less than a dozen are in cultivation today.

Epacris is the Australian analogue of the South African Erica and in general appearance—habit, foliage and flowers—they are singularly alike. The Epacris are found in the scrub and alongside streams growing among low bushes. They are seldom more than a few feet tall and have slender, rigid, often erect, branches, small spinescent leaves and axillary tubular flowers either white, pink or red. They were among the first plants introduced into Europe from Eastern Australia but are now less often seen than their beauty warrants. The finest is the variable *E. impressa* which is abundant in the southeast corner from South Australia to Tasmania. The type has pink flowers, the var. *parviflora* white, and var. *longiflora* red and white flowers. With smaller flowers there are in cultivation *E. purpurascens* with pink flowers, *E. breviflora* and *E. obtusifolia* both with white flowers. The plant grown as *E. hyacinthiflora*, of which there are several color forms, seems to be nothing more than a race of *E. impressa*, whilst that known as *E. hybrida superba* is a mixture of several varieties. It is very doubtful if there are any genuine hybrids.

Of the related and much larger genus Leucopogon, readily known by its small, white, bearded flowers, a few species only are in cultivation. The best known are *L. Richei* and *L. lanceolatus*. Two other genera related to Epacris and worthy of mention are Richea and Dracophyllum. Out of blossom these strongly resemble in foliage and habit some of our Yuccas. Of the eight species of Richea perhaps the best known are *R. dracophylla* and *R. pandanifolia*. There are four species of Dracophyllum and *D. Fitz-*

geraldii, endemic on Lord Howe Island, is the giant of the genus.

A twiggy shrub with saucer-shaped rose-colored flowers is *Bauera rubioides* often seen as a pot-plant in greenhouses. This plant forms interminable thickets in Tasmania and elsewhere. Several species of the fragrant-leafed Prostanthera with pretty purple flowers are in cultivation and so, too, are *Correa speciosa* and *C. Backhousiana* with pendent, tubular, red-tipped yellow or greenish flowers.

Of climbing plants Eastern Australia has contributed very little to our gardens. Nevertheless, I must not omit mention of *Swainsona galegifolia.* This favorite, with its dainty foliage, pretty white, pink, red and purple-colored flowers on erect axillary racemes, has been long established in our gardens.

Of herbs with conspicuous flowers Eastern Australia is not especially well off. In the dry areas there are carpets of Everlastings but they are not so luxuriant as those of Western Australia. The genus Ptilotus (better known as Trichinium), related to Amaranthus, is widely spread in the region of low rainfall and, growing gregariously, blankets wide spaces with color. They are low plants with pink, purple or yellowish flowers in dense cylindrical spikes and are commonly known as Silky Heads. Of the seventy-eight known species, Bailey mentions one east Australian species (*Trichinium exaltatum*) and the west Australian *T. Manglesii*.

Belonging to the Amaryllis family are several fine Eastern Australian plants. Among them are eleven species of Crinum, one of which, the dainty *C. flaccidum*, grows inland in all the states except Tasmania. Some of the others are tropical. In the drier regions grow *Calostemma luteum* and *C. purpureum* with prominent straight stamen-filaments, and on the coast the Brisbane Lily (*Eurycles Cunninghamii*). The latter has rounded leaves and white, fragrant Eucharis-like flowers in umbels on scapes 2 feet high. Very remarkable are the large growing Spear Lilies (*Doryanthes Palmeri* and *D. excelsa*) with broad bright green Yucca-like leaves and tall, flowering stems terminating in massive inflorescences of crimson flowers. But of this ilk the Lily family claims the peer with its fascinatingly lovely Christmas Bells (Blandfordia). These have hanging bell-shaped flowers in umbels on stalks a foot and more high. In color the flowers are bright orange-red to red-brown and are edged with yellow. Of the four species *B. flammea* and its variety *princeps* are the most ornamental. One, *B. grandiflora*, is purely Tasmanian. The Dianellas with their narrow swordlike leaves are also worthy of note on account of their charming blue berries.

Terrestrial Orchids, some of them with very dainty and beautiful flowers, are plentiful and some epiphytic ones, including several Dendrobiums, are found within our purview although none of these are meritorious garden plants. North of the tropic and outside our region are found such well-known and valued species as *Dendrobium speciosum, D. superbiens, D. bigibbum* and *D. Phalaenopsis.*

In the rain-forests Ferns in variety luxuriate. Two Tree-ferns are especially noteworthy, namely, the familiar *Dicksonia antarctica* and *Alsophila elegans;* and to these same rain-forests we owe the noble *Platycerium grande* and *P. alcicorne,* respectively known as the Elk and Stag Horn Ferns.

AUSTRALIA

CHAPTER XX.

A Marvellous Dowry

HE Australian flora as known today exceeds 10,700 species which belong to over 1400 genera, and four-fifths of the species are not known to grow wild elsewhere in the world. Of this vast number probably not more than a thousand have been introduced to northern gardens and but few of these have gained a permanent foothold in cultivation. Toward the close of the Eighteenth Century and through the first five decades of the Nineteenth there was much activity in the field of plant collecting in Australia. Seeds and plants were constantly being transmitted to Europe, chiefly to England, and as they flowered these were figured in the magazines and gardening periodicals of the time. It is only by turning over the pages of these old publications that we are able to realize the work that was done at that period.

Australia is a land of sunshine and it is easy to understand that under the gray skies of northern Europe the cultivation of many Australian plants proved well-nigh impossible, and their number dwindled annually. In the sunny Mediterranean regions conditions were more favorable and there a number of these introductions found a permanent home. Had a keen garden spirit flourished in those days in California and other warm parts of this country the story would have been different. In these lands a vast number of Australian plants would luxuriate out-of-doors. Unfortunately now California and elsewhere are ready to receive these plants comparatively few are available and they must be reintroduced from Australia.

In botanical gardens, such as Kew, fair collections of these plants are maintained with difficulty but in the trade and in private gardens they are rare and our generation knows nothing of New Holland plants compared with that of our fathers. As very few of these plants are hardy in northern Europe and the colder parts of this country, I do not think they will come back into cultivation there. The expense of maintaining glass is so great today as to largely prohibit this. Furthermore, there have been discovered so many beautiful hardy plants that our outdoor gardens are crowded and there is no room for tender, difficult subjects.

In lands of sunshine like southern California and

the Mediterranean region the story is different and it
is in such lands that Australian plants are both desirable and necessary.   There the climatic conditions
will suit a majority of the most brilliant flowered
and desirable Australian species since they approxi-
mate closely to those of the southern continent. Take
that remarkable family so well-named Proteaceae
which is represented in Australia by thirty-four genera and about 679 species.   How many have we in
this country? Maybe tucked away in collections a
couple of dozen might be mustered but in general cultivation I can think of only one—*Grevillea robusta*
—and this raised annually from seeds to grow as a
pot-plant for decorative work and summer bedding
on account of its elegant and graceful foliage. There
are more than 190 other species of Grevillea in Australia.   Again, let us consider Banksia with its erect
cone-like, greenish white, yellow to scarlet flowers.
This is one of the most strikingly handsome and remarkable groups of woody plants.   There have been
discovered some sixty species of which about half-a-
dozen are slightly known in Californian gardens, but
not one is commonly grown.   A majority of the
Proteaceae—truly a family of protean and wonderful plants—have brilliantly colored inflorescences

and are worthy of a place in all gardens where the climate is congenial.

Of all the vast array of Australian plants only about a dozen genera have permanently established themselves among us and become familiar plants in our greenhouses or out-of-doors in our warmer, sunny lands. Eucalyptus is Australia's grandest, as it is also her most characteristic, group of trees. It is also her greatest gift to other lands. This gift belongs more to the domain of forestry than to that of horticulture but every garden-lover who has been privileged to see the Red-flowered Eucalyptus (*E. ficifolia*) in blossom will gratefully acknowledge his indebtedness to Australia for this tree. There are several others (*E. torquata, E. macrocarpa, E. erythronema, E. pyriformis, E. Preissiana* and *E. erythrocorys* with brilliantly colored flowers worthy of a place in every Californian garden. In general the Eucalypts are the most widely and abundantly planted of all broad-leaf trees and every year sees larger areas devoted to them. Their value to forestry in many countries is inestimable and yet their planting has only just begun. In lands like South Africa, where trees and timber are badly needed, millions of acres are awaiting the tree planter.

I have mentioned one use of *Grevillea robusta* but

it should be added that as an ornamental tree it is abundantly grown in the tropics of both hemispheres and, further, it is of much value to planters as a shade tree for Coffee, Cocoa and other crops. In Australia itself the future will see this tree grown in quantity for paper-pulp.

For horticultural purposes pure and simple two Palms (*Kentia Belmoreana* and *K. Fosteriana*) from Lord Howe Island, and *Araucaria excelsa* from Norfolk Island—both outlying dependencies of New South Wales—have become indispensable to us, and the export of seeds is an important source of income to the inhabitants of those remote islands. Norfolk Island is volcanic and the Araucaria flourishes on the sea-cliffs. In the adult stage it is far from being the neat-shaped tree with tabular tiers of branches so familiar to us. The continental *A. Cunninghamii* is equally handsome though rather less formal in habit, yet it has never become popular in our gardens. The noble Elk's Horn Fern (*Platycerium grande*) and its close relative the Stag's Horn Fern (*P. alcicorne*), well-known to Fern-lovers, are both Australian. They are common epiphytes in Queensland and contiguous parts of northeastern New South Wales. The first-named is partial to the more tropical brush while the Stag's Horn is frequently seen in the scrub, especially on *Casuarina glauca*. One of our most familiar Tree-ferns (*Dicksonia antarctica*) is Australian, being particularly abundant in Tasmania and southwest Victoria. Another from the warmer parts of New South Wales and Queensland is *Alsophila australis*, discovered and introduced in 1820.

It is in Acacias that our gardens are richest in Australian species. Nearly every sort we grow hails from the southern continent. The delicate and charming *A. pubescens*, the lovely *A. Baileyana*, the vigorous *A. dealbata* and *A. melanoxylon*, the graceful *A. longifolia* and *A. pulchra*, the glaucous-gray *A. cultriformis* and *A. podalyriaefolia*, the neat compact *A. Drummondii* and the familiar green and prickly *A. armata* all came from there.

Among our favorite pot-plants we count Boronias and such as the fragrant *B. megastigma*, the bright colored *B. elatior* and *B. heterophylla* are well established in our affections. So too are various Pimeleas, with their crown of white and rose-colored blossoms, and the Chorizemas with small holly-like leaves and curious orange and red flowers in slender racemes. The free-flowering Epacris, with slender, rigid, erect stems, small prickly leaves and bright colored tubular Heath-like flowers are much less grown than their beauty merits. Some thirty species are known and all are lovely though only a few are known to our gardens. These plants are peculiarly Australian being unknown in any other land. We occasionally see an odd plant of the Bottle-brush (Callistemon) and of the Needle-bush (Hakea), but they have made no mark on our gardens.

Of Australian herbs only the Swan River Daisy (*Brachycome iberidifolia*) and the Pink Everlasting (*Helipterum Manglesii*)—both annuals—are really familiar tenants of ours. The lovely Christmas Bells with large, conspicuous orange-red to reddish brown and yellow flowers are, unfortunately, but little known to us. These belong to the genus Blandfordia of which four species are known, the finest being *B. flammea*, introduced into Europe in 1850 from Sydney Botanic Gardens.

The expert will of course recall other Australian plants known to him in rare collections but this does not alter the fact that little more than a dozen genera are today popular and established in our gardens. The total number is ridiculously small and the gardens of California alone could accommodate thousands. To stock our gardens we claim of the world its best floral treasures. This work is intended to show whence and how came the gems we prize and to indicate others no less worthy of our possession. For certain parts of this country Australia holds much in store.

CHAPTER XXI.

My Lady Acacia

THE plants of Australia are noted for their gay and brilliant colored inflorescences and in elegance and charm, fragrance and beauty, none excel the Acacias. Wattle is the name in Australia applied to Acacias, and the Wattle-bloom is the national floral emblem of that land. It appears on the national coat of arms, on postal notes and on postage stamps; also in Australia there is a Wattle Day League, the object of which is to promote and increase the interest of the people in their national flower. In etymological dictionaries Wattle is defined as a twig or flexible rod; a hurdle made of such rods; a rod laid on a roof to support the thatch. When used as a verb it signifies to bind with twigs; to twist or interweave twigs one with another; to plait, to form of plaited twigs. It is from the Anglo-Saxon *Watel* or *Watul*, a hurdle. In the early days of Australian colonization the branches of Acacias and of other twiggy trees were used in the manner indicated in the erection of various structures. In the process of time the word

165

Wattle in Australia has become restricted to Acacia with which it is now virtually synonymous.

Wattles are found in every Australian state from the coast to the arid interior, in swamps and on dry mountain slopes, alongside of rivers and on the plains. More than 400 species have been described and Acacia is the largest genus of native Australian plants. In size Acacias vary from tiny shrubs a few inches high (*A. Baueri*) to large trees 100 feet and more tall (*A. melanoxylon*), but most of them are small trees or shrubs a few feet high. They form the under-storey in the Eucalyptus forests, and in the drier parts they grow gregariously and are frequently the dominant type of vegetation. The Mulga (*A. aneura*) and Myall (*A. pendula*) are two species characteristic of the dry regions and give their names to two types of scrub prevalent over much of the continent. Acacias are found in all kinds of soil and under all sorts of conditions; one species (*A. sophorae*) in Tasmania luxuriates in pure sea-sand, holding down the dunes and is quite indifferent to salt water. The west Australian *A. saligna* also grows in similar situations. This species has been introduced into South Africa and is naturalized on the sandy flats near Cape Town where it is a great boon

for, with *Pinus pinaster*, it has gone far toward re-
claiming these wastes into residential sites.

The species of Acacia fall naturally into two great
groups. One named "Bipinnatae," has normal, pin-
nately divided leaves present throughout the life of
the plant. These feathery leaves vary greatly in size
and their day and night positions are different. During the daytime the leaflets are spread horizontally
but at night they rise up and arrange themselves next
to one another like the leaves of a closed book. Their
profiles are toward the night sky and the loss of heat
by radiation is reduced to a minimum. These
"sleep-movements" are brought about by the direct
action of certain special tissues. With a falling
temperature and a diminishing intensity of light the
cells lose water and shrink, causing the leaves to assume their night-position; with a rising temperature
and an increasing intensity of light they absorb water
and so regain their turgidity and cause the leaves to
assume the day-position. In the other group true
leaves are present only in the seedling stage, being
quickly superseded by flattened petioles of varied
shape which perform the functions of leaves. These
flattened petioles or leaf-stalks are called phyllodes,
and all Acacias furnished with them are called "Phyl-

lodinous." This section is almost exclusively confined to Australia and Polynesia.

Bipinnate Acacias grow wild in America, Africa and India and are popularly but erroneously known as "Mimosas." In Australia grow only some thirty species of this section yet among them are such gems of the group as *A. Baileyana, A. pubescens, A. decurrens* and *A. dealbata.* In blossom these are shower bouquets of yellow, and with their slender branches, elegant, feather-like foliage and wealth of fragrant flowers they are entrancingly lovely. Their naturally spreading branches are weighted down with the yellow masses of flowers and form inviting canopies under which to linger. To see *A. decurrens* 40 or 50 feet high with its profusion of yellow blossoms contrasted by the feathery foliage in the month of August, is a sight not to be forgotten. The umbrella-like crown of other species is specially inviting and such as *A. pubescens* seems to be calling all in holiday mood to rest within its bower. On the lawn in sunny lands, or in cool conservatories where the winters are long, what is more inviting than a seat beneath the feathery green and golden canopy of these joyous Wattles? There is a peculiar softness and delicacy about both foliage and blossom and a warmth in the honey-laden perfume. As an Australian child described them, "Sprays of Wattle flowers are like my pussy, so fluffy and warm that I love to hug them."

There is no doubt for graceful beauty, for cutting and general decorative purposes the Australian Mimosas are the pick of the whole genus. They never resent cutting; when in blossom they may be sheared back to the main stem, every leafy branch may be cut off and the plant will furnish a new crown equally well laden with flowers the ensuing season. Also on the whole they are the toughest of the tribe. Of course no Acacia will withstand long-sustained freezing but an occasional degree or so of frost does them no harm. Bailey's Acacia is perhaps the hardiest and at Cootamundra, its home in New South Wales, sharp frosts are not unknown. In South Australia it is reported to have been unscathed by a snap of sixteen degrees of frost. However, readers are not to infer that Acacias are hardy plants, but, many species are much hardier than is commonly supposed and an odd degree or so of frost is not harmful. In eastern North America and in northern Europe they are cool greenhouse plants and for the winter garden ideal subjects. They flourish best in the comfortable living temperature enjoyed by the average white person. The humid temperature necessary for the well-being

of Palms, Ferns and Orchids is not to the liking of
the Australian Acacias any more than to us. A cool
dry air, a living atmosphere, is the requisite and this is
added reason why they should be more widely grown
in our conservatories. In California and other warm
lands they are of course quite at home out-of-doors
and a great variety can be enjoyed. There is, however, one point to be remembered, many species are
surface rooting, the famous *A. Baileyana* especially,
and, moreover, their branches are apt to split and
break. Therefore they should be planted out of
reach of strong winds and pruning should not be
forgotten.

A hundred years ago New Holland plants, as they
were called, enjoyed a great reputation in northern
gardens and of these plants Acacias, thanks to their
adaptability, have held their own better than others.
A few sorts are still grown in quantity by florists, and
tucked away in California and Europe there are a
great many species. Probably very few of those introduced have actually been lost but many are rare in
cultivation.

The horticultural records are so imperfect that it
is impossible to discover when many exotics were
introduced into this country. The first record which
I have been able to find of Australian Acacias in

America is in the "Magazine of Horticulture" III. p. 115 (1837), where J. Lowell of Boston tells of having *Acacia armata* and *A. longifolia* in flower in his greenhouse. In the same periodical, volume IV. p. 114 (1838), it is stated that Marshall P. Wilder at Hawthorne Grove had in blossom in March *A. spectabilis*, *A. conspicua* and *A. pubescens*. These facts are interesting since they prove both the enterprize of garden-lovers and the interest that was taken in Acacias nearly a century ago. That *A. pubescens* was growing here in 1838 is particularly noteworthy in view of its rarity today, and that it was considered one of the best, agrees with the opinion still held. The history of this most exquisite Acacia is worth recording. A native of New South Wales, it was sent soon after the Colony was founded to Sir Joseph Banks, who received it in 1790. Under the name of *Mimosa pubescens* it is figured by Ventenat in his "Jardin de La Malmaison" t. 21 (1803), the plate having been prepared from a drawing by the famous artist Redouté. Unfortunately the branch is figured in an upright position and gives no proper idea of the graceful beauty of the plant. Much better is the figure in the "Botanical Magazine," (t. 1263) where it is truthfully described as " one of the greatest ornaments of the greenhouse and with a fragrance of fresh made meadow-hay." The writer also adds that "it is difficult to propagate except by seeds." This fact explains why it has remained so rare a plant in gardens for a century and more. It will root though tardily from cuttings but with moderate ease it can be grafted on such species as *A. dealbata.* This fact was demonstrated by that master-hand, the late Jackson Dawson, who, in August, 1912, successfully grafted seven plants on the Silver Wattle and on March, 1914, when a photograph was taken, the plants were over 6 feet tall. Whether the feat had been earlier accomplished in Europe there is no means of knowing but this is the first on record here in America.

The phyllodinous Acacias are multitudinous and all are good garden plants—some, of course, are more beautiful than others but down to the homely Mulga they are worthy. A few of the Mimosas as named above are exquisite—apart—but the rank and file bear no comparison as garden plants to their phyllodinous kinsmen. The balloons of gold, exhibited by such species as *A. hakeoides, A. decora,* and scores of others, leave an impression on the mind of the most permanent character. The pin-heads and tassels of flowers are either solitary, panicled and axillary, or, both axillary and terminal; often fathom-long, slender branches are decked with flowers and whole bushes and trees are simply one blaze of fragrant yellow. In some species the plants are merely peppered with yellow balls, in others they are immersed in them. Truly, the season of the Wattle-blossom in Australia is lavish in color and beauty, and the air is laden with the soft, warm fragrance of a world of flowers.

In the absence of spreading petals the bundles of stamen-filaments serve as perches for insects to rest upon and suck the nectar. The pollen is unprotected, indicating that the season of blossoms in their home-lands is one when dry air and sunshine prevail. The fruit is a dry pod varying greatly in size and shape and is of great importance in classifying the species. The pod opens to liberate the seeds which are oval and flattened, often more or less lunate in shape and in color of varying shades of brown to black. In a few species (*A. homalophylla* and *A. cyclops,* for example) the seeds hang from the ripe pods on encircling orange-red stalks which serve to attract birds and aid in their seed dispersal. The seeds, which are hard—often very hard—and retain their vitality if not attacked by insects for a great many years, vegetate rapidly after fire has swept over their homeland. In raising Acacias from seeds germination is greatly accelerated by steeping for a night in almost boiling water before sowing in the soil. A common method in Australia is to scatter the seeds among the hot ashes of a burnt rubbish pile where they germinate freely and quickly.

In the size, shape and form of the phyllodia, Acacias differ greatly one from another and are easily divisible into several groups. In one the phyllodes are leathery in texture, elongate, more or less oblong, from 4 inches to a foot long, often curved in outline, light to dark green, usually broadest above the middle and narrowed at the base and abruptly so at apex. To this group belong A. neriifolia, A. saligna, A. melanoxylon, A. retinoides, A. decora, A. cyano-phylla, A. binervata, A. penninervis, A. gladiiformis, A. cyclops—all with globose flower heads; A. pycnantha with ovoid heads, and A. longifolia, A. sophorae and A. linearis with tassel-like inflorescences; with more narrow phyllodes and pin-heads of flowers A. fimbriata, A. accola and A. leprosa, and, with catkinate inflorescence, A. acuminata. In another group the phyllodia are narrow and spinescent at the apex and either flattened as in A. calami-folia, A. verticillata and A. Riceana, or rounded as in A. colletioides and A. ephedroides. In large group the phyllodes are thin and membranous in texture, less than 2 inches long, more or less ascending in position, sometimes tipped with a short spine and in shape varying from oblong-oval or oblong to obovoid and hatchet-shape. Usually such phyllodes are dark green, and here belong *A. obliqua, A. acinacea, A. Howittii, A. imbricata, A. brachybotrya, A. hastata, A. pravissima,* and *A. armata* and its variety *paradoxa* (Kangaroo Thorns) with stipular prickles; sorts with blue-gray glaucous phyllodes are *A. cultriformis, A. vestita* and *A. podalyriaefolia.* In *A. extensa* the shoots are slender and flattened and the phyllodes hardly distinguishable in form from the branchlets. A further modification is seen in *A. alata* and *A. diptera* where the stem is broadly winged and spreading phyllodia are absent. The modification the phyllodia undergo is extraordinary, and the most casual observer may find much of interest in Acacias quite apart from the beauty of their blossoms.

The most useful of Australian Acacias are *A. melanoxylon* for its wood, *A. decurrens* for its bark, and *A. aneura* as cattle fodder in times of drought. For usefulness and beauty combined the Black Wattle (*A. decurrens*), the Silver Wattle (*A. dealbata*) and the South Australian Golden Wattle (*A. pycnantha*) with its bark richest in tanning, probably rank first. For sheer beauty it is not possible to say which is best.

The people of South Australia would acclaim their own *A. pycnantha*, emblem of the Wattle League, those of Sydney *A. decurrens* and *A. longifolia*, those of Brisbane *A. podalyriaefolia*, of Hobart *A. Riceana*, of Melbourne *A. pravissima* and those of Perth *A. saligna*. If a referendum of the whole of Australia were taken probably the exquisite Cootamundra Wattle (*A. Baileyana*) would head the list. So it probably would in Europe and North America, although the south of France would shout for the Silver Wattle (*A. dealbata*) and eastern North America for the lovely *A. pubescens*. A variety of opinions—honest ones—make for progress and among the wealth of Australian Acacias there is beauty enough to satisfy the most fastidious tastes.

The economic value of Acacias is considerable. Many species furnish timber of great value. Perhaps the most famous is the Blackwood (*A. melanoxylon*), native of southeastern Australia and Tasmania. In the rich alluvial bottom lands this is a tree of great size, sometimes more than 100 feet tall, with a trunk 20 feet or more in girth and a massive, blackish green billowy crown. The wood is chocolate-colored and often beautifully figured. It is highly valued in furniture and cabinet-work. It grows well in southern India, on the highlands of equatorial Africa, in

Natal and other parts of South Africa, and promises to be the most valuable of all Acacias for forestry purposes in these lands.

Such species as the Eummung (*A. salicina*), Mountain Hickory (*A. penninervis*), Hickory Wattle (*A. Bakeri*), Scrub Hickory (*A. Maidenii*), Brush Ironbark (*A. aulacocarpa*), Ironwood Wattle (*A. excelsa*), Gidgee (*A. pendula*), and Raspberry-jam Wood (*A. acuminata*) have woods of considerable value for a variety of purposes. Perhaps the greatest use of all these woods is for cutting veneers. When burning, such wood as that of Myall, Yarran, Brijalow and Raspberry-jam are pleasantly fragrant. The Raspberry-jam is worthy of extended notice. It is a low, broad-topped tree native of Western Australia where it forms pure woods. The branches are slender, the flowers in short axillary tassels, and the wood, which has the identical odor of raspberry-jam, is well-nigh everlasting in the ground. This species is partial to strong soil and is indicative of good wheat land. In times of drought the branchlets and phyllodes are eaten by stock. The same to a greater degree is true of the Mulga (*A. aneura*), one of the homeliest members of the family but what it lacks in good looks it makes up in good works. Its dry as well as fresh branchlets and phyllodes are much relished by stock and in times of great drought this Acacia has often saved the farmer from the ruinous loss of all his animals. A gray-green scrawny, low tree, the Mulga is widely distributed through the drier parts of Australia and is often reduced to a small shrub.

The bark of many Acacias is a valuable tanning agent and certain species are cultivated in parts of the world expressly for their bark. The richest in tanning is the bark of *A. pycnantha,* the south Australian Golden Wattle, but that most widely grown for the purpose is *A. decurrens* and its variety *mollis* respectively the Black and Green Wattle. In Natal the industry is a flourishing one. This country enjoys a virtual monopoly of the industry and the tree seems to be peculiarly at home in that part of South Africa.

CHAPTER XXII.

They Who Paid the Price

ET US enquire a little into the history of the coming of Australian plants to northern gardens. The agencies have been various and all sorts and conditions of men have played a part. It is the province of the taxonomic botanist to describe and fix names to the plants of the world and often he, too, has won them from the wilds to our gardens. A good deal of the material has come to hand through devious channels, and much of the work of introduction has been done by men of great enthusiasm, often well versed in practical knowledge of the art and craft of gardening but of little learning; men who gave heed to little, save the plants they loved, and of themselves thought not at all; men of obscure origin who flashed for a brief while across the garden-world then disappeared without trace; men of unknown birth whose place and time of death are unrecorded. To such men—a gallant army—our gardens are largely indebted and we who love our flowers may well be grateful to these hardy, forceful pioneers.

It has already been stated that the buccaneer and

180

navigator—Dampier—the first Englishman to visit
Australia, in 1688 and 1699, collected a few plants
which are still preserved at Oxford University. The
famous Sir Joseph Banks and his companion, Dr.
Solander, collected nearly 1,000 species at Botany
Bay and other places on the east coast. Banks introduced *Casuarina torulosa* from New South Wales,
and this was the first Australian plant to reach
Europe. It was growing in Kew Gardens in 1772.
Archibald Menzies collected at King George's Sound,
and then followed Robert Brown with the botanical
artist, Ferdinand Bauer. These collections formed
the basis of Brown's "Prodromus." The first French
expedition—that of D'Entrecasteaux in 1792—had
the botanist Labillardière on board; that of Baudin,
in 1800, Leschenault, and that of Freycinet was accompanied by Gaudichaud. With these botanists
were gardener-assistants and many plants were introduced into France. Australia was, indeed, fortunate
not only in the number but in the caliber of the
botanists who early visited her new-found shores and
well and truly laid the keel of her botany. The
assistants to Banks and Solander, four in number
(Messrs. Buchan, Parkinson, Reynold and Spon-
ing), all died on the voyage. The vessel was wrecked
and nearly lost at Cape Tribulation in Queensland,

and Captain Cook, Banks and Solander were stricken with fever at Batavia in Java and barely escaped death.

The material on which the French botanist L'Heritier based the genus Eucalyptus was collected by David Nelson, a young Kew Gardener whom Banks was instrumental in sending with Cook on his third voyage, at Adventure Bay, Tasmania, in January, 1777. Nelson afterwards accompanied Captain Bligh on the ship "Bounty" to Tahiti for the purpose of introducing the Breadfruit tree into the West Indies. After the mutiny he was placed in an open boat with Bligh and others by the mutineers. This boat was successfully sailed 3000 miles to Timor, where Nelson died from exposure and hardship in 1789. Peter Good, another young gardener from Kew, who accompanied Robert Brown, died of dysentery at Sydney in 1802. Good introduced from Western Australia, in 1802, the pleasing *Acacia pulchella* and the well-known *A. armata;* also the first Chorizemas (*C. ilicifolium* and *C. rhombeum*), *Banksia littoralis, B. coccinea, Hakea suaveolens, Dryandra formosa, D. floribunda* and six other species, all raised in Kew in 1803.

Messrs. Brown and Bauer returned safely to England without mishap in 1805, but Captain Flinders, in attempting to sail from Sydney to England in a twenty-nine-ton boat, was forced to put into Mauritius (then French) for ship repairs and was imprisoned there for over six years in consequence of war between France and England. He ultimately reached England but died of a broken heart in 1814, at the early age of forty years.

Archibald Menzies sent *Banksia grandis, B. attenuata* and *B. verticillata* to Kew, where they were growing in 1794, having been collected at King George's Sound in 1791. In 1802, *Banksia latifolia* was introduced from New South Wales by Thomas Hoy and, in 1810, no fewer than twenty species of these remarkable plants were in cultivation in England—more than there are today.

Many notable plants were introduced by the nurserymen, Messrs. Lee & Kennedy, as early as 1790. Among them were Grevilleas (*G. sericea* and *G. buxifolia*), and in 1794, the first Boronia (*B. pinnata*). Others of about the same date (1788-90) are accorded to Banks, as for example, *Callistemon lanceolata* and *C. saligna, Hakea acicularis, Grevillea linearis* and the lovely *Acacia pubescens*. In 1793, Banks received the first Pimelea (*P. linifolia*). It is probable that the earlier of these were sent by Denis Considen, assistant-surgeon to the colony and a pro-

tégé of Banks, who returned to England in 1792,
others by David Burton, a gardener sent out by
Banks in 1791 and accidentally killed in 1792, and
by Colonel Paterson, who held a military appointment in New South Wales previous to 1794.
Colonel Paterson was afterwards (1804-1810)
Lieutenant-Governor of Tasmania. He took a great
interest in botany and is commemorated by the genus
Patersonia, the austral analogue of our northern Iris.
A tree (*Lagunaria Patersonii*), much planted in
Australia and elsewhere but endemic in Norfolk
Island, also bears his name. I think it more than
likely that he sent, or Considen took, the first plants
of *Araucaria excelsa* from Norfolk Island to Banks,
who received them in 1793.

It is interesting to note that *Acacia pubescens* was
introduced so long ago as 1790, yet it is still very
rare in gardens. It was, in fact, the second species introduced, the first being *A. verticillata* in 1780,
which was sent from Tasmania by David Nelson.
The first Banksias introduced were *B. ericifolia* and
B. integrifolia in 1788 from New South Wales, by
Thomas Watson. The two Banksias are mentioned
by the elder Aiton in his famous "Hortus Kewensis"
published in 1789. The only other Australian
plants mentioned in this work are *Casuarina torulosa*,

introduced from New South Wales by Banks in 1772, *C. stricta* from the same region by Messrs. Lee & Kennedy in 1775, Nelson's Acacia, under the name of *Mimosa verticillata*, and *Eucalyptus obliqua* attributed to Tobias Furneaux in 1774. Captain Furneaux commanded the "Adventure" in Captain Cook's second voyage and called at Tasmania in February, 1773, the place being named Adventure Bay after the ship. As we have stated, the genus was founded on material collected at Adventure Bay by David Nelson in 1777 on Cook's third voyage. If Aiton's statement be true then *E. obliqua* is not only the type of the genus but also the first species introduced and this prior to the founding of the genus and the naming of this species from Nelson's material by L'Heritier.

In 1800, at the instance of Banks, George Caley arrived in New South Wales where he explored and collected until 1810. He introduced a number of plants, including *Acacia podalyriaefolia* and *Epacris purpurascens,* the first of the genus to reach our gardens in 1803. The well-known Fern, *Platycerium alcicorne,* he sent home in 1808. Later, Caley became Curator of the Botanic Garden at St. Vincent, West Indies, resigning the end of 1822. He was the son of a Yorkshire horse-dealer and seems to have been somewhat uncouth in appearance and eccentric in manner though of sterling honesty and loyal to the few friends he made.

The dawn of the Nineteenth Century saw the garden merit of Australian plants generally recognized in Europe, and particularly in England. In 1803, *Epacris longifolia,* and in 1804, *E. microphylla* and *E. obtusifolia* were introduced from New South Wales by Loddiges of Hackney. From these and Caley's *E. purpurascens,* sprang an interesting group of greenhouse plants, today, alas! but rarely seen. In 1823-25 and again in 1829, William Baxter, a gardener, collected round King George's Sound and in South Australia for the Clapton Nursery, then owned by Messrs. Makay, and made that nursery famous for New Holland plants. Among other plants he introduced *Epacris impressa* from South Australia.

The most illustrious name in the history of plant exploration in Australia is that of Allan Cunningham, one of the greatest plant hunters of all times. Of Scotch descent, he was born at Wimbledon, near London, in 1791, and received a liberal education; his father intending him for the law, but he preferred gardening and obtained employment at Kew under the elder Aiton. In 1814, Allan Cunningham was sent to Brazil where he collected for two years, and as Sir Joseph Banks wrote "did credit to the expedition and honor to the Royal Garden." He was next appointed to New South Wales and landed at Port Jackson on December 21, 1816. From then until 1831 he was assiduously employed in exploring and plant collecting round the coast on vessels and into the far interior. He suffered dangers and hardships of every kind and amassed rich collections.

In 1826, Cunningham visited New Zealand, where he remained nearly half a year and endeared himself greatly to the Maoris. In 1832, the post of Colonial Botanist was offered to him but this he declined in favor of his younger brother, Richard. Two years afterwards this brother was murdered by the Blacks and the appointment being again offered was accepted by Allan. He reached Sydney on the 12th of February, 1837. The post not being agreeable to him he resigned a few months later and resumed his plant exploration work. But the hardships he had suffered had done their work, he died of tuberculosis on June 27, 1839, "A martyr to geographical exploration and botanic science, in the forty-eighth year of his age." His remains have found a worthy resting place in the Botanic Garden, Sydney, among the plants he had loved too well.

There is no more worthy and honored name among the band of plant hunters than that of Allan Cunningham. Many plants have been named for him but to my mind there is none more fitting than that lusty, noble evergreen, the truly magnificent *Araucaria Cunninghamii*—the Hoop Pine—which he discovered in 1827, near Brisbane, together with *Grevillea robusta*. His writings are few and the present generation, even in Australia, know little of the debt we owe to the noble-hearted Allan Cunningham.

The first Colonial Botanist was Charles Fraser, who had been a soldier in a regiment commanded by Governor Macquarie. Fraser was appointed in 1828 and proved an indefatigable explorer and collector. He visited Swan River, Moreton Bay and Tasmania and enriched our gardens with a goodly number of plants. Among them I may mention *Platycerium grande*, discovered by Allan Cunningham in 1820 and introduced into the Glasgow Botanic Garden by Fraser in 1829. His report on the Swan River had much to do with the founding of the colony there, and it was he who established the Botanic Garden at Sydney. When on an expedition to collect plants especially for this garden he was stricken with a fatal illness in 1831. He had gone with carts to Bathurst for living plants, and on the return journey was taken ill some twenty miles from Parramatta which he reached in a very debilitated state and died there two days later.

In 1829, James Drummond went to Perth as Curator of the Botanic Garden and remained in Western Australia until his death in 1863. He sent home seeds of a great variety of plants and probably did more to make the flora of that country known than any other man. He was the elder brother of Thomas Drummond, who collected so much in Texas and for whom the well-known *Phlox Drummondii* is named. James was born about 1784, and had an excellent training for the work he took up, having been Curator of the Botanic Garden, Cork, from 1809. His specimens and seeds were sent to Robert Brown, Sir William Hooker and Dr. Lindley, and many plants were received in Kew and other gardens. Among the plants introduced by James Drummond are *Acacia Drummondii*, *Leschenaultia grandiflora*, *L. laricina*, *L. biloba*, *Pimelea spectabilis*, *Boronia heterophylla* and *Chorizema varium*. The brothers Drummond are commemorated by the monotypic and endemic Australian plant, *Drummondita ericoides*.

For the "purpose of discharging a religious duty"

James Backhouse of the nursery firm of that name at York, England, landed in Australia in 1832 and spent six years there. He visited Tasmania, New South Wales, South Australia and Swan River and collected wherever he went. He is commemorated by the Myrtaceous genus Backhousia of which the best known species is *B. myrtifolia* of New South Wales.

I may conclude this account of collectors with Ronald Campbell Gunn, who did so much to make known the flora of Tasmania. Born at Capetown in 1808, he went to Tasmania in 1830 and died there in 1881. Gunn collected assiduously during his whole life and made known to science many new plants. He is commemorated by a number of plants, of which I may instance *Eucalyptus Gunnii*, one of the hardiest of the genus, and *Nothofagus Gunnii*, the only deciduous tree of Tasmania.

CHAPTER XXIII.

Wisdom of Men

 WISE administration caused a Botanic Garden to be founded in the capital city of each Australian state. These Gardens from their inception have served as collecting and distributing centres of plant material, and have naturally had a leading part in building up the knowledge of the Australian flora the world enjoys today. They have sent plants far and wide and have played an enormous part in the creating and fostering of the garden spirit in the southern continent. The best of the floral gems of the tropics and of the northern Hemisphere they introduced and disseminated into Australian gardens. When I visited these Botanic Gardens and saw how splendidly they are patronized by the public I asked myself time and time again, "Why has America no such flourishing institutions so well established in the affections of the public?" The only answer that suggested itself I refrain from writing down.

In Sydney, the Mother City of Australia, the first Botanic Garden was established by Charles Fraser about 1829. The site includes that of the first plats

of wheat and other cereals and vegetables, planted
under the authority of Captain Phillip when he un-
furled his flag at Sydney Cove on January 26, 1788,
and established the colony of New South Wales.
For over a century the Sydney Botanic Garden has
been intimately bound up with the material welfare
of Australia and is classic ground. Its area includes
the site of the first farm where corn was grown for
the infant colony, where fruit-trees of all kinds—
apples, oranges, olives, grapes, bananas—were first
acclimatised, where it was shown that cotton and
innumerable other economic plants could be grown
successfully in New South Wales, while by means of
wardian cases and glass houses it was the means of
establishing and propagating valuable tropical economic plants for what is now Queensland and
Northern Australia. The garden has had ups and
downs and its various directors have at times been
hard pressed but for more than half a century it has
been well-stocked with a rich collection of the
choicest plants from all quarters of the globe. In
1847, Charles Moore was appointed Superintendent
and remained in control until 1896. Moore introduced many plants to cultivation, including *Kentia
Belmoreana* and *K. Fosteriana* from Lord Howe
Island in 1869. He was succeeded by the late J. H.

Maiden, F. R. S., and erstwhile Dean of Australian botanists, who enlarged the activities of the gardens on all sides and made Sydney the headquarters of Australian Botany.

The only other garden I have space to mention is that of Melbourne, established in 1845. It was re-modelled with great skill and thirty acres were added by W. R. Guilfoyle, appointed Director in 1873. The site enjoys good soil and the garden boasts a wonderful collection of plants zealously maintained. Melbourne is famous to garden-lovers for the association of the great Dr. (afterward Sir) Ferdinand von Mueller, who was appointed Colonial Botanist to Victoria in 1852. Mueller travelled and collected extensively and added enormously to the knowledge to Australian flora. His writings are multitudinous and laid the foundation for the proper study of many important genera, including that of Eucalyptus and Acacia. He had correspondents all over the world and distributed seeds and specimens far and wide. During his lifetime he was the dominant figure in Australian botany. The herbarium he amassed at Melbourne is a monument to his industry and devo-tion to the science he so long adorned. He died in October, 1896.

The hour is late and my tale must end though it is

scarce begun.   Verily it is only an odd word or two of the story.   Through it all looms the figure of that great, good man, Sir Joseph Banks, scientist and explorer, patron and devotee of Botany and Horticulture, who, from his return to England in 1771 to his death in 1820, never lost an opportunity of adding Australian plants to the gardens of the North.   Co-discoverer with Captain Cook of New South Wales, he labored for the founding and afterwards for the advancement of the Colony and well earned the title, affectionately bestowed upon him by a grateful people, of "Father of Australia."

TASMANIA

CHAPTER XXIV.

Isle of Enchantment

HE close of the Sixteenth Century saw the Dutch virtual masters of the Old World seas and intent on establishing commercial supremacy throughout the eastern tropics. The Dutch East India Company was established in 1602, with headquarters of trade at Batavia whence the government was wont to dispatch expeditions in the hope of extending the trade and dominion of the Dutch Flag. The unknown South Land, which had existed as a kind of myth since classical times, became the Terra Australis Incognita, a vaguely imagined continent, dreamed of, adumbrated and finally sighted by a succession of navigators. The mythical land became real and tangible and desire to know its real extent and value stirred the breasts of the Dutch traders.

In 1642, Governor Van Dieman, a man of enterprise and shrewdness, determined upon an expedition to explore the great unknown South Land and, if possible, discover a new trade route to South

America.   One, Abel Janszoon Tasman, who was born of obscure parents in the village of Luytjegoot, Groningen, in 1603, was appointed in command. On August 4, 1642, Tasman set out from Batavia in the "Heemskerck," a vessel of 200 tons, with the flyboat "Zeehan" of less burden in company. Mauritius was reached on September 5th, and a stay of a month was made to recondition the ships and take on supplies for their adventurous voyage.   Sailing in a southerly direction the southwestern tip of Australia was rounded and then voyaging eastward they sighted, on November 24th, land which can be easily identified as the mountains at the back of Macquarie Harbor on the west coast of Tasmania.   Thus Van Dieman's Land, as Tasman named it, was seen for the first time.   The vessels sailed round the south coast and anchored off what is now known as Forestier's Peninsula.   The surf prevented Tasman himself landing but a ship's carpenter swam ashore and planted the flag.   Continuing to sail to the eastward, New Zealand was discovered and a bloody encounter with the Maoris took place.   Tasman then put his ships about and sailing north by west returned to Batavia through the straits north of New Guinea, arriving home on June 15, 1643, with the loss of fourteen men.   This historic voyage proved

Australia to be an island and that a possible route to South America existed, but the Dutch appear to have made no use of this knowledge and their enterprise in the southern seas subsided almost completely after this voyage of discovery.

After a lapse of 140 years Tasmania was again visited. This was a period of great rivalry between France and Britain, and the story of the rediscovery and later colonization of Tasmania is the story of rival French and English discoverers sailing, ostensibly in the interests of science but really to extend their empires. In 1770, Captain Cook discovered New South Wales, and in 1772 a French Captain, Marion du Fresne, rediscovered Van Dieman's Land and saw the native people for the first time. On his third voyage Captain Cook, in 1777, anchored in Adventure Bay and landed on Bruny Island. In 1792, Admiral Bruny D'Entrecasteaux with the naturalist, Labillardière, visited Tasmania and surveyed the Derwent Estuary and, in 1797, George Bass, an English naval surgeon, crossed from Australia in an open whale boat and proved Tasmania to be an island.

At the close of the American War of Independence a scheme was mooted to find a home for English loyalists in Australia but it was Canada that received them. At the close of the Eighteenth Century, fearing that France might take action England decided to settle and so annex Tasmania. A few convicts and soldiers with Lieutenant Bowen in charge were sent from Sydney, New South Wales, and settled at Risdon on the Derwent in 1803. The site proved unsatisfactory and the next year Hobart Town was founded, from which date the history of Tasmania as an English Colony begins.

Tasmania is a small heart-shaped island situated off the southeast corner of Australia and separated from the mainland by the Bass Straits, which are about 200 miles wide. Part of the Commonwealth of Australia and much the smallest of the six component States, it has a total area of 26,215 square miles, being slightly smaller than New Hampshire, Vermont and Massachusetts combined. Like those states it is a region of mountains, lakes and rivers, of forests and fine scenery.

It consists mainly of a central plateau bounded on the west and southwest by mountain masses and shelving away on the north and east to undulating sandstone plains. The plateau is called the Central Lake Plateau from the presence of five large lakes which give rise to the principal rivers of the island. The plateau is of volcanic origin, being composed of diabase or greenstone, and has an altitude of from 2500 to 3300 feet. It is more or less ringed by isolated flat-topped mountains of similar rock formation ranging in height from 3500 to 5000 feet above sea-level.

The west coast is of granite, gneiss and Pre-cambrian schists reared into rugged mountains whose summits are 4500 feet high. This west coast is exposed to the full sweep of the Southern Ocean gales, which, unintermittently blow from west to east and know no break in land between Tasmania and Cape Horn. The storm-worn west coast and central plateau are drenched with heavy rainfall which reaches its highest annual precipitation (over 165 inches) on Mt. Read. Winter and summer the wind blows incessantly, with constant cyclonic disturbances irrespective of season, and snowstorms happen on the high tablelands every month in the year. The storm-driven clouds cause such excessive rainfall that the foothills and upper slopes of the west coast and central plateau are clothed with a dense mixed forest, only the extreme summits being bare.

The east coast is sheltered and dry with a total annual rainfall varying from about twenty-six to thirty-three inches. The north and northwest portions of Tasmania are also more or less protected from the prevailing west winds but are exposed during summer to hot north winds from Australia, and the vegetation consequently approximates to the drier Australian type. Hobart, the capital city, is situated on the south coast on the banks of the Derwent River and beneath Mt. Wellington, whose plateau-summit is 4200 feet above the sea. Thus sheltered, Hobart enjoys a genial, dry climate, the annual rainfall being about twenty-four inches and the mean temperature about 54°F. with a yearly range of 15° F.

CHAPTER XXV.

Here and There

APPROACHED Tasmania by sea from Sydney, New South Wales. Early on St. Patrick's morning of the year 1921, land was sighted and by ten o'clock in the morning the vessel rounded Cape Pillar, the island's most southeastern point. This high, bold cape is of basalt columns, always impressive with their organ-pipe-like arrangement. Sailing fairly close to the southern shore fine scenery was unfolded. The coast is much indented and the arms of the sea forcibly remind one of Scotland's lochs. Sugar-loaf hills are common and hills and dales, woodland and water blend in one enchanted whole. Rounding a bend, the estuary of the Derwent was entered and by two o'clock the vessel was moored alongside a wharf at Hobart Town. Everything was placid and peaceful and this impression remained to the end. Hobart is but a small place stretching along the river front and backward on sloping land toward Mt. Wellington, its guardian from the boisterous westerly winds. Woodland of Eucalyptus, alas, much damaged by fire, stretches upward to the frowning basaltic cliffs, the organ-pipes of the mountain.

A smiling welcome and good accommodation were found at Hadley's Hotel. Hospitality rules in Tasmania and visitors are made to feel themselves at home immediately. My visit on behalf of the Arnold Arboretum of Harvard University was expressly for the purpose of looking over the forest wealth and gaining an insight into the flora in general. The Government presented me with a railway pass and the Conservator of Forests accompanied me on several extended tours. Motor cars made distances short and travel pleasant. Thanks to these courtesies and abounding hospitality from farmer, lumberman, mine-owner and others, my visit was not only professionally most profitable but a round of delight.

From the scenic point of view the most interesting trip from Hobart is to Tasman Peninsula and Port Arthur, some fifty miles by motor. The peninsula is of basalt and presents many interesting features. At Eaglehawk Neck there is a tessellated pavement of worn basalt columns suggesting the Giant's Causeway in northern Ireland. The curving shores of Pirate's Bay, with *Acacia sophorae* binding down the sand, sparkle in the bright sunshine. Beyond loom cliffs of basalt and on the headland the Devil's

Kitchen, Blow-hole and Tasman Arch demand inspection. These remarkable phenomena have been caused by ceaseless tides breaking down and bursting fissures through the basalt columns. They are weird and fearsome scenes of jagged rock and hissing, roaring, moaning waters. Chained as it were, yet ever lashing themselves in fury, the waters break, tear and erode the rocks into black caverns and seemingly bottomless pits. Wandering amid these scenes I gathered many pretty flowers of Eucalyptus, Epacris, Pimelea, Acacia and the charming blue-fruited Billardiera, a slender twining plant. From Eaglehawk Neck twelve miles through fine Eucalyptus forests with abundant undergrowth of Tree-ferns brings one to Port Arthur of sinister history.

Another pleasant trip is along the banks of the Derwent River to Russell Falls some forty-eight miles. Passing through New Norfolk with its fine Hop gardens, one pauses to visit the Salmon ponds at the Government fish hatchery. Here are planted many exotic plants, and magnificent specimens of Babylon Willow and Monterey Cypress are to be seen. As showing how rapidly trees grow in this favored isle, I may mention a specimen of Monterey Cypress sixty years of age with a trunk measuring 14 feet in girth.

The Russell Falls are situated on the edge of the
National Park, an area of 38,000 acres on the central plateau. The falls are about 100 feet high, in
three tiers, garnished with lovely Tree-ferns (*Dicksonia antarctica*) with broad, fathom-long, arching
fronds of rich green topping massive black-brown
trunks. All around is virgin forest of Eucalyptus
and Southern Beech (*Nothofagus Cunninghamii*).
The entrance to the forest around the falls is guarded
by groves of splendid *Eucalyptus obliqua* whose
clean boles clad with fibrous gray bark are 80 to 100
feet tall. Deeper in the forest are giant *Eucalyptus
regnans* with stoutly buttressed trunks. A rich
undergrowth of Ferns and Mosses, the fragrant air
and pleasant noise of falling waters make the Russell
Falls an enchanting entrance to Tasmania's National
Park.

Of different character is a tour to Port Cygnet,
westward from Hobart along the south coast and
back by Brown's River. This is over low mountain
shoulders and hills and through the Apple region of
the Huon Valley. Once forested with huge Eucalyptus much of the land has been cleared for agriculture.
One may regret the disappearance of giant trees but
is forced to admire the abundant apple harvest which
rivals that of the best parts of this country. But the

Eucalyptus is not easily conquered, axe and fire may destroy this monarch but his seeds, preserved by Mother Earth, strive hard to replenish the ground with another forest and they succeed wherever the farmer neglects his orchards and fields for a few years.

Hobart Town has its sandy beaches and pleasant shore-resorts and not a few delightful trips by steamer through sheltered waters may be had. Adventure Bay is such a trip and hither I hied for, to a botanist, it is a sacred spot. Here it was that David Nelson, who was attached to Captain Cook's third expedition, in 1777 gathered specimens of a tree which were taken to Europe; on this material L'Heritier founded the genus Eucalyptus, naming the species *E. obliqua.* I sought the oldest trees and gathered specimens, musing on the destiny of fate that had brought me to this spot hallowed to the memory of a fellow Kewite.

Hobart is the capital of Tasmania but in commerce and size is rivalled by Launceston on the Tamar River in the north, and between the two towns there is not a little jealousy. The rival towns are connected by a railway which passes through grazing country skirting the Lake Plateau. Merino sheep and dairying are important industries through these Midlands, as the region is called. From

Launceston westward a railway extends to Burnie,
a small shipping port. This is through rich agricultural land where dairy farming and orcharding
prosper, the region being probably the best for the
purpose in this island. From Burnie a railway goes
south over the highlands to Strahan at the head of
Macquarie Harbor, from whence a short line leads to
the mining center of Queenstown.

From Burnie I made a pleasant motor trip of about
seventy miles to the Arthur River to see a virgin
Blackwood swamp. The Blackwood (*Acacia melanoxylon*) is one of the most valuable timber trees of
the island, yielding a dark red-brown, close-grained
wood much used in cabinet-making, church-furni-
ture, office-fittings, billiard-tables and musical instru-
ments. The tree luxuriates in rich, moist black soils
and grows associated with Nothofagus, Paper-bark
trees (Melaleuca) and a few Eucalyptus. Under such
conditions it is the dominant tree and regenerates
freely. Its maximum size is about 100 feet in height
with a straight trunk 12 feet in girth and a broad,
billowy crown. The northwest corner of Tasmania
strongly reminded me of South Australia. There
grow curious Grass-trees with shock-like heads of
narrow, brittle leaves and erect spear-like rods of
white flowers, Paper-bark trees with white layers of

bark flapping in the breeze; park-like are the forests of Eucalyptus and the plains are bright with colored flowers all suggestive of South Australian scenery. We passed through several of the curious Button-grass plains which are peculiar to Tasmania. These are flat areas of peat-bogs clothed solely with Button-grass (*Sphaerocephala*), which grows from 3 to 4 feet tall and is topped by a button-like inflorescence. Nothing else grows there, or, so little as not to affect the general appearance of these dismal areas which extend mile upon mile.

From Burnie I took the Emu Bay Railway south through forested and mining country to Strahan. Much of the journey is through mountainous virgin country, steep and well-wooded. In the gullies grow Leatherwood (*Eucryphia Billardieri*), a tree 60 feet tall and 5 feet in girth of trunk. Above these Eucalyptus (*E. Deligatensis* chiefly) clothes large areas of the mountainside with lofty trees. Higher still the polished leafed *E. vernicosa* has its home, and with it the most alpine of Tasmania's tree Eucalyptus (*E. Gunnii*) is noticeable on account of its conspicuous dull yellow-barked trunks. It yields the hardest of all Tasmanian timbers. Through the railway cuttings Silver Wattle (*Acacia dealbata*) clothes the banks and I was told that like the railway it was a newcomer. However, in former times it grew there but was driven out by the Southern Beech and other trees; the construction work gave the buried seeds a chance to germinate. In the gullies Ferns in great variety form a lush growth with the noble *Dicksonia antarctica,* a tree up to 20 feet, king of all.

Strahan I found a tiny village, approached through aggressive sand-dunes, storm swept in keeping with its reputation. A boat trip to the Gordon River had been arranged for us but angry Macquarie Harbor with towering waves lashed by a strong gale said no. Strahan is the port of supply and shipping for the Mt. Lyell mines around Queenstown, which are reached by a mountain railway fifteen miles in length. And a wondrously pretty journey it is with the clear water of King River on one side and forested mountains all around. The trees are mostly bright green with a few Eucalyptus in evidence, Southern Beech dominates, with narrow crowned Sassafras (*Atherosperma moschatum*) and Huon Pine, with pale green pendent branchlets, prominent above a dense undergrowth of wondrous *Cyathea Cunninghamii* and other Tree-ferns. Queenstown nestles in a gully among the mountains and all around is stark and bare with débris vomited from the mines piled high on all sides—a scene of desolation although vastly productive in mineral wealth, chiefly low-grade copper ores.

The heart of Tasmania is a central plateau from 2500 to 3300 feet above sea-level. Its main feature is a series of large lakes, from which the rivers take their rise and radiate north and south through the Island. The Great Lake is now being utilized as a source of hydro-electric power and, later, others also will be turned to the same use. I reached the Great Lake by motor from the town of Deloraine after a pleasant forenoon's ride. Ascending through rich arable and pastoral lands, we passed through Eucalyptus and scrub woodlands over the rim of the Great Western range and descended to the plateau through patches of King William Pine to the banks of the Lake. The scenery is subalpine in spite of the low altitude and is accentuated by the flat-topped mountains, isolated and bare of forests on their summits and some 1500 feet higher than the Lake. Great Lake is a fine piece of water with verdure to its very edge; placid and deep blue its loveliness seemed ethereal. It is typical of the whole series, beautiful to look upon but cold, and the vegetation tells plainly of the rigorous climate of the region. Though comparatively low the growth is dense and impenetrable without an axe.

CHAPTER XXVI.

Midst Blue-gums and Tree-ferns

THE Tasmanian flora is essentially east Australian even as the island itself was once an integral part of that continent. Owing to the great variation in climate, rainfall in particular, the flora presents great variation in richness in the different parts of the island, and the contrast in appearance between that of the west and east coasts is nothing short of amazing.

Eucalyptus, Blackwood, Southern Beech and various Conifers are the principal timber trees of Tasmania. The finest Eucalyptus forests were and their remnants still are in the southern part of the island. They compare favorably with the Gippsland forests of Victoria and like them support a rich undergrowth in response to the heavy precipitation enjoyed. Unlike our northern trees Eucalyptus cast but the minimum amount of shade, owing to the fact that the leaves hang and present only their edges to the sun's direct rays. There are three distinct Eucalyptus types readily distinguished by their barks: the Gums, which shed their bark each year and in consequence have stark, smooth boles; the Blue Gum (*Eucalyptus globulus*) is a familiar example; Stringybarks, characterized by a gray fibrous persistent bark, not very thick and only slightly fissured—*E. obliqua* is a type; Ironbarks which have dark almost black, deeply furrowed, rugged persistent bark—*E. sideroxylon* is an example. A fourth type, descriptively named Gumtop Stringybark, may be recognized, of which *E. Deligatensis* is a Tasmanian type. Apart from these striking bark characters the Eucalyptus are much alike. With great trunks of uniform thickness and height and branching only at the crown, they stand in serried ranks, noble and inspiring to look upon. Above Geeveston I stood within the portals of virgin forest and marvelled at its richness, pure stands of *E. obliqua* averaging 200 feet in height with clean trunks 20 feet in girth and 120 feet to the first branch. Beneath them as a second storey grew Southern Beech (*Nothofagus Cunninghamii*), Celery-top Pine (*Phyllocladus rhomboidalis*) and a few other trees. The rich undergrowth was largely of Ferns among which noble *Dicksonia antarctica* lorded. This impressive Tree-fern lines the sides of the mountain streams, its massive trunk swathed in Mosses, Liverworts and Filmy-ferns. So, too, are all the fallen rotting trunks and old stumps, the forest floor a luxuriant fernery, from which are upthrust the massive Eucalyptus trunks crowned with a canopy of polished foliage. The flowers of the Eucalyptus are rich in honey and are much frequented by bright colored, honey-seeking birds, of which Tasmania boasts many.

In the wetter places Swamp Gum (*E. regnans*) dominates with towering straight, white trunks buttressed at the base. The Blue Gum (*E. globulus*) is particular as to soil, demanding the best, and usually occupies pockets all alone. Some years ago Tasmania supplied the Admiralty Dock at Dover, England, with a large number of piles, each 100 feet long and squared 20 inches by 20 inches at each end. These were of Blue Gum and the man who filled the contract told me in Hobart that his difficulty was not in finding the trees but in loading the piles on to the ship!

Tasmania knows no Palm, Pandanus, Cordyline or other tree-form of Monocotyledon but in *Richea pandanifolia* she boasts a slender tree that simulates these types. This Richea is often 40 feet tall, of uniform stem thickness with sedge-like leaves from the base upward, remarkable for their longevity and persistence on the trunk. It is a distant relative of our own Rhododendron.

Eastward from the central plateau as the rainfall

decreases the character of the forests changes. Eucalyptus remain the dominant trees but are smaller of size, grow farther apart, are much less impressive to the eye and the rich undergrowth of green pellucid Fern vanishes. The whole character of the forests is open and park-like with undergrowth of coarse grasses, low, often thorny bushes, and the country reminds one of South Australia around Adelaide.

The forests of the west coast with its nearly incessant precipitation are dense, jungle-like and bright green in appearance. This forest is not rich in species and is characterized less by its height than by its density of growth. This density is aggravated by the peculiar behavior of the Horizontal Wood (*Anodopetalum biglandulosum*) whose limp branches, falling to the ground, send up secondary shoots from every joint and form inextricable masses over wide areas. The region is extremely rugged and steep with a dense undergrowth of Ferns and Mosses clothing rocks and dead trees, and these features, with Horizontal Wood added, make the west coast forests almost impenetrable. Southern Beech (*Nothofagus Cunninghamii*) in many parts is dominant. Of moderate size this is a much-branched tree with very numerous small Myrtle-like leaves casting a heavy shade. With it grows fragrant Sassafras (*Atheros-*

perma moschatum) with smooth bark, whorled branches and shining leaves, Leatherwood (*Eucryphia Billardieri*) with lovely flowers, Laurel (*Anopterus glandulosus*) with handsome racemose white blossoms, and the graceful Palm-like *Richea pandanifolia* protrudes its head at every vantage point. With these broad-leaf trees, either scattered or in small groves, grow the five valuable Conifers of Tasmania; the handsome Huon Pine (*Dacrydium Franklinii*) with drooping branches in youth and a spreading crown at maturity, dense crowned Celery-top Pine (*Phyllocladus rhomboidalis*) with black-green, wedge-shaped, notched leaves and bark rich in tannin, King William and Red Pine (*Athrotaxis selaginoides, A. cupressoides* and *A. laxiflora*) with straight, brown trunks and oblong crowns. Midway up the mountains Eucalyptus occur but not in the majesty that marks the southern forests. The dominance of Southern Beech and the dense undergrowth remind one of the rain-forests of the west coast of the South Island of New Zealand.

The Central Lake plateau is covered with a low dense forest-thicket as may be expected of a region where hurricanes and blizzards sweep at any season of the year. There are no glaciers or permanent snowfields in Tasmania, where not one peak exceeds

5000 feet in altitude, but the constant strong winds and frequent storms throughout the year reduce vegetation to the minimum in height. Alpine herbs are rare and in their stead reign low shrubs tenacious of life and capable of withstanding the austere climatic conditions which prevail on highland and peak. Taken in its entirety the vegetation of Tasmania is an epitome of that of the combined Australian states of South Australia, Victoria and New South Wales and its outstanding features are the towering Eucalyptus, the dense undergrowth and the wealth of Ferns and Mosses. It is poor in endemic species and in herbs with conspicuous flowers, and with a few unimportant exceptions its trees and shrubs are all evergreen.

Remote from us is Tasmania, Gem of the Antipodes, with its indented coasts and mountain walls lashed by the furies of the Southern Seas. Extinct are its palaeolithic aboriginal inhabitants, slashed are its virgin forests and its pristine beauty in part is shorn. Much of its land has been brought into service of man, its mineral wealth is under toll and its lakes harnessed to supply power for the use of the people who have made the island their abiding home. Since the island assumed its present name it has ever known peace, and prosperity in a quiet way has followed in the wake.   Beautiful it is with a mantle of green forests, clear water streams and lakes, bold cliffs and rugged mountains—an enchanted isle where rest and quiet reign remote from the strife and enmity, the rush and noise of northern lands.   So may you remain Tasmania is the prayer of one visitor!

NEW ZEALAND

CHAPTER XXVII.

Queen of the Southern Seas

EW ZEALAND, Queen of the Southern Seas, is totally unlike Australia and the differences are much greater than the some 1200 miles of ocean that separates them would appear to warrant. No Eucalyptus, Acacia, Grass-tree, Banksia, Melaleuca, Casuarina, Callitris nor Cycad, the dominant types of Australian forest and bush, are native of New Zealand. A typical Australian genus that is well represented in New Zealand is Pimela, which boasts fifteen species. Its presence in such quantities is curious and interesting. Leptospermum is also characteristically Australian and, although two species only occur in New Zealand, the plants are so abundant as to form a dominant feature of the unforested areas. But, to take a wider view, it is remarkable that Proteaceae, which is one of the most prominent families of the Australian flora, should be represented in New Zealand by two trees only, namely, *Persoonia toru* and *Knightia excelsa,* both endemic. In Australia grow many species of Persoonia but Knightia does not grow there, although two species are known from New Caledonia. It would appear then that a few Australian waifs and strays occur in New Zealand even as such New Zealand types as Nothofagus and Phyllocladus maintain a bare foothold in eastern Australia.

Gray-green foliage does not characterize New Zealand's trees, neither is gorgeous blossom her floristic feature. Quite the contrary. New Zealand's forest mantle is of the greenest and in appearance partakes more after that of Oregon, Washington and British Columbia than of her sister-land. Her flora is largely peculiar to the country and its real relationship is with that of the temperate parts of South America on the one hand, with that of the islands of Malaysia on the other, and only very slightly with that of eastern Australia. If we are to visualize New Zealand's plants we must forget entirely Australia's characteristic vegetation. Green, intense green, is the keynote of New Zealand. Her trees are almost entirely evergreen, her forests are dense and impenetrable with rampant climbers and the lushest of Fern undergrowth. On her lofty mountains she boasts a rich and remarkable alpine flora and, in the south, many curious types adapted to arid conditions, but most of the country is, or rather was, densely forested, with Tree-ferns, Filmy-ferns, Ferns of a hundred sorts in billions. Green forests with a dense, dripping undergrowth of Ferns and Mosses of all sizes is the lasting impression one has of this southern land. But if this be the dominant feature it is not the whole picture. As my learned friend, Dr. L. Cockayne, points out in the opening chapter of his fascinating book, "New Zealand Plants and Their Story," "New Zealand can boast the largest Buttercup in the world, a Forget-me-not with leaves as big as those of the Rhubarb, a tree Speedwell, 40 feet in height, the smallest member of the Pine-family, tree-like Daisies, plants of the Carrot-family with stiff leaves sharp as bayonets, Mosses more than a foot tall, and, those strange anomalies of the plant-world, the Vegetable Sheep." These and others shall be told of but first let us consider the country itself.

New Zealand is situated well south in the vast Pacific Ocean. It consists of two large (North and South) islands, a much smaller one (Stewart Island) and many lesser islands and islets. In all its total area is about 105,000 square miles, which is slightly larger than the state of Colorado. It was discovered by Abel Janszoon Tasman who after discovering Tasmania sailed eastward and on October 13, 1642, came upon the northern part of the North Island, which he took for part of a great southern continent. After a bloody scrimmage with the Maoris, Tasman put to sea and sailed away to Batavia. Afterward, until the coming of Captain Cook on October 8, 1769, New Zealand and its Maoris, who are considered to have settled there about 1350, A. D., were undisturbed by the white man's voyagings. Landing first at Poverty Bay in the north, Cook circumnavigated the land and proved it to be an island. On January 31, 1770, the British flag was hoisted and Cook annexed the country to the British Crown.

On this memorable voyage was Sir Joseph Banks with Dr. Solander and other assistants, and at the different points of landing they collected over 300 species, the first gathering made of New Zealand plants. In 1773, Captain Cook again visited New Zealand and with him the botanists Forster, father and son, who collected more plants. In 1791 came Captain Vancouver with surgeon-botanist Menzies, who gathered in quantity Mosses and Liverworts. The French in 1824 and again in 1827, with D'Urville in command and René Lesson as naturalist, visited and made collections; in 1840 another French expedition sailed for New Zealand with M. E. Raoul as surgeon-botanist, who added largely to the knowledge of the flora. Then in 1825 came enterprising Charles Fraser, in 1826 that prince of plant hunters, Allan Cunningham, and in 1833 his ill-fated brother Richard, all of whom carried away many living plants to the Sydney Botanic Gardens. Afterward came the great botanist Joseph D. Hooker, also missionaries and others interested in botany and, later, men born in the land or settlers there began a thorough examination of the whole flora. In the 157 years that have elapsed since Captain Cook's epochal visit, New Zealand has risen to wealth and sistership in the British Commonwealth and the study of her flora has been steadily pursued with the result that, today, it is known to approach 1800 species.

New Zealand is a very mountainous country, a land of splendid scenery. Much of the North Island is volcanic and hot springs and geysers are a feature of its central part, the Rotorua region, where placid lakes of lovely waters rimmed with forests, quiet streams, rushing torrents and falling waters lend enchantment to the land. West of the lake region are volcanic peaks from 8000 to 9000 feet high. The South Island is traversed throughout its entire length by a range whose highest peaks are clad with snow eternal. On the west side, which is steep and precipitous and penetrated by long, narrow fiords or sounds, the mountains rise abruptly to culminate in snow peaks, of which Mt. Cook is 12,349 feet high. On some of the mountains the glaciers are easily accessible so much so in fact that they may be reached by motor car! On the eastern side of this snowy, glaciated range steep-sided valleys lead down to deep lakes and open out into plains that extend down to the sea. Those of Canterbury are famous for their sheep farms whilst those of Otago to the south are arid and the home of many curious plants.

I landed at Auckland and after a trip to the Kauri forests to the north went south to Rotorua and later to Wellington. Crossing to Christchurch on the South Island I travelled south to the Bluff with side trips to Queenstown, on Lake Wakatipu, and to Mussel Beach; returning to Christchurch I crossed to Hokitika on the west coast and then travelled north to Nelson, whence I took ship to Wellington. Through the extreme courtesy of the New Zealand government I enjoyed free travelling facilities through the land. The officials of the Forestry Service did everything to make my visit a success and their efforts were admirably seconded by botanists, lumbermen and farmers who, one and all, spared themselves nothing likely to add to my pleasure and enjoyment. Of the fragrant recollections I retain of New Zealand, none is pleasanter than that of the mutual respect I found among Whites and Maoris one for the other. There, at least, alien races live together in amity and good fellowship, equal in political status, tolerant and neighborly toward each other.

CHAPTER XXVIII.

Forest Wealth

EW ZEALAND before its settlement by white men was, for the most part, densely clothed with mixed rain-forest in which old types of Taxads and Conifers were the dominant trees, but axe and fire have in less than a century played sad havoc and, today, much of the land is a jungle of Bracken Fern (*Pteridium aquilinum* var. *esculentum*), Manuka (*Leptospermum scoparium* and *L. ericoides*), with naturalized European Gorse (*Ulex europeus*) and Bramble (*Rubus fruticosus*). Originally all the wetter parts where tree growth was possible were covered with pure forests of Taxads and Conifers but, save on the west coast of the South Island and excepting the Kauri in the north, these old types have long since been unable to compete successfully against the intrusion of the more modern broadleaf trees. Even without the destructive intervention of the white man it is evident that in time, another 500 years perhaps, broadleaf trees will completely dominate the forests and the Taxads and Conifers will have become virtually extinct over the greater part of New

Zealand. Today for the most part the Taxads and
Conifers, except the Kauri-pine, are scattered thinly
through the forests and are crowded on every side by
dicotyledonous trees.

The undergrowth, except in pure Nothofagus
forests, is very dense, almost impenetrable, and consists of broadleaf shrubs and small trees and Ferns.
Climbers, though few in species, are numerically rich
and epiphytes, like Astelia, crowd the treetops. The
higher Cryptograms, especially Ferns, are extraordinarily abundant. Stately Tree-ferns abound and
lovely Filmy-ferns drape wet rocks, tree trunks and
branches. Club-mosses are plentiful and in the
densest shade of dripping forest the exquisite *Todea
superba* luxuriates. There are few deciduous leafed
trees in the New Zealand forest and only a small
number have conspicuous flowers.

The forests of the North Island are obviously
older than those of the South, where the glaciers are
even now slowly retreating, but a majority of the
trees are distributed through the whole of the country from north to south, including Stewart Island.
In swampy rather open places the Cabbage Tree
(*Cordyline australis*) and the New Zealand Flax
(*Phormium tenax*) are common. The margins of
ponds and shallow lakes are crowded with a species

of Typha. The flat areas of the thermal region beyond Rotorua are clothed with Manuka (*Leptospermum scoparium* and *L. ericoides*), Bracken Fern, and
a narrow-leafed species of Dracophyllum. The treeless Canterbury plains, now arable land or pastures
for sheep and cattle, were formerly covered with Tus-
sack grasses, as are much of the adjacent mountain
ranges and the arid plateau of south Otago. In the
alpine areas in rich variety grow all sorts of curious
plants including many herbs with lovely flowers. The
Rimu (*Dacrydium cupressinum*), Totara (*Podocarpus totara*), White-pine (*P. dacrydioides*), Matai
(*P. spicata*), Miro (*P. ferruginea*) and the Kauri-
pine (*Agathis australis*) are the most valuable timber trees.

The Kauri is monarch of New Zealand's forests
and one of the noblest of existing trees. Once it
formed magnificent forests from a little south of the
present city of Auckland northward, but ruthless
felling and burning have virtually destroyed this tree
so far as commercial lumbering is concerned. There
remain only an indifferent State forest at Waipoua,
where the Kauri is the chief tree, and a National Park
of some 700 acres in parts pure stands of Kauri.
This valuable Conifer is a strikingly handsome tree
and its wood is easily worked and exceedingly dur-

able. In young trees the branches are numerous, short and slender and form a narrow pyramidal crown. By means of a layer of special tissue these weak branches are shed after the manner of leaves on deciduous trees and leave a clean trunk quite free of knots. The adult tree is very different in appearance, the crown being open, flattened and fairly wide-spreading. The trunk is clean, cylindric with no taper and from 50 to 75 feet high and is clothed with gray bark which, peeling off in flakes of no particular shape, form a large mound round the base of the tree. Owing to the smooth, scaling bark no climbing plant hides the beauty of the trunks, which stand above the forest undergrowth like granite pillars in a vast cathedral. The undergrowth is fairly dense but not tall and the Kauri trees tower far above the Tree-ferns and associate plants. The largest specimen I saw was about 37 feet in girth and the tallest 150 feet high. The average trees are from 100 to 120 feet tall and from 15 to 20 feet in girth with clean trunks from 60 to 75 feet high. The largest recorded tree had a trunk-girth of 66 feet and there are stories of even larger trees. Owing to the perfectly cylindrical character of the trunk the Kauri yields for its size a greater quantity of timber than any other tree. The well-known kauri gum exudes freely from wounds and collects in the axils of the branches; it is also found beneath the ground where ancient forests of the tree grew.

The Totara, Rimu, White-pine, Matai and Miro are widely distributed through the length and breadth of New Zealand. The Totara is being rapidly cut down in all accessible places and the Matai and Miro do not seem to be really common trees anywhere, but the Rimu and White-pine are still plentiful and on the west coast of the South Island form extensive and fairly pure forests. When young the Rimu is a beautiful tree with long, pendent, light green branch-lets but when old is merely a tall pole supporting a small mop-like crown. In fact the same is true of all the chief soft-wood trees of New Zealand, when old, except the Kauri. A young Totara resembles the common Yew but its foliage is a lighter green; young White-pine is very like the Red Cedar (*Juniperus virginiana*). The White-pine is best on alluvial river flats where it averages from 120 to 140 feet in height and has a mast-like trunk buttressed at the base. Its pure white wood is valued for making butter boxes and for this purpose is exported in quantity to Australia. The wood of Rimu, Matai and Miro are used in general carpentry and furniture-making. That of Totara lasts well in the ground and is valued for telegraph poles and the like. So, too, is that of the Silver-pine (*Dacrydium Colensoi*), a much rarer tree apparently confined to the west coast. Two species of Libocedrus are useful timber trees and so, too, are the Phyllocladus. *Libocedrus Doniana* is not found much south of the city of Auckland but *L. Bidwillii* is widespread from the southern part of the North Island southward.

The broadleaf trees are not considered of much commercial value though the wood of many is durable and will ultimately be in request. Two of the most aggressive of these trees on the North Island are *Beilschmiedia tarairi* and *Knightia excelsa*. Very interesting are the various Ratas (*Metrosideros robusta* and other species), which in thick forests often commence life as epiphytes on the Taxads, Conifers and other types of trees. For a time they behave as ordinary root climbers but when their roots reach the ground their strangle-hold on the supporting tree intensifies and the Rata grows completely round, enclosing and killing its former host. Often the same species of Rata grow and behave as do normal trees from their youth onward. The wood is heavy, hard and tough and is used for cross-arms on telegraph and telephone poles.

But next to the Gymnosperms the most interest-

ing trees are the species of Nothofagus or Southern
Beech, which in many parts of the South Island and
the more southerly parts of the North Island form
dense, pure forests of considerable extent. Especially
is this the case in the drier parts, in stony gullies and
on the tops of moderately high mountains; in some
places they even descend to sea-level. The bark is
more like that of the common Hornbeam than that
of our northern Beech. The Nothofagus regenerate
readily and singularly resemble the Hemlock (*Tsuga
canadensis*) in general appearance. I saw only small
or moderately large trees but was told of specimens
100 feet tall and 25 feet in girth of trunk. They
grow thickly together and in pure forests allow no
undergrowth. Quite often patches of Nothofagus
occur in the ordinary mixed forests but whether
under these conditions they are intrusive or vestigial
it is difficult to determine.

The forests of New Zealand are not only full of
interest but highly instructive phylogenetically since
their cycle is clearly manifest. The types are old,
very old, even many of the broadleafed trees, and the
country itself is but a remnant of a vast continent
which once linked together South America on the one
hand and Tasmania and eastern Australia on the
other. First in the dim and distant past above the

Mosses, Ferns and other Cryptogams rose the Taxads and the Kauri, soon to be followed by other Conifers. Possibly the very species existing today, but in so far as the sequence of forest types is concerned it does not matter whether it were they or their ancestral types. For a period these trees, unchallenged, forested all the suitable land. Later came the broadleaf dicotyledonous trees, the struggle for supremacy began and today the broadleaf usurpers hold the field.

There are no Cycads in New Zealand and the arborescent Monocotyledons are limited to a few small trees, which include two Cordylines (*Cordyline australis* and *C. indivisa*) conspicuous with their shock-like heads and flaring masses of white flowers, and one Palm (*Rhopalostylis sapida*), known as the Nikau. To these may be added the scandent *Freycinetia Banksii* which scales to the tops of the highest trees.

In the dense under shade of the present forests, Taxads and Conifers cannot grow. The seeds often germinate but the seedling plants die after a short struggle. The broadleaf trees on the other hand regenerate readily. Where the Taxads and Conifers flourish the soil is humus and peat from 3 to 6 feet deep and it is seldom that the roots descend into the mineralized subsoil. When planted in ordinary soil they grow very slowly. The broadleaf trees grow under shade and a variety of soil conditions and their roots ramify in all directions. I pulled up seedlings and small plants of every Taxad and Conifer I came across and in each case found the roots clothed with tubercles. I did the same with the broadleaf trees but found no tubercles present. My attention was directed to the presence of tubercles on the roots of Taxads and Conifers by Captain L. MacIntosh Ellis, the Director of the Forests. Later I found that their presence was known to others but the significance does not appear to have been grasped by anyone except by the Director of Forests and no investigation of this phenomenon had been attempted. The tubercles are analogous with those on the roots of leguminous plants and in all probability the Bacteria break up the raw humic acids and convert them into readily available food salts. It is a simple and beautiful case of symbiosis but I have no knowledge of such in our northern Taxads and Conifers, though it is known in the case of the Alders and a few other broadleaf trees other than Leguminoseae with which it is general. This discovery is important for, if I am right in my conclusions, the organisms within the tubercles are controlling factors in the rate of growth of the Taxads and Conifers of New Zealand. As evidence let us consider what happens in the forests. The lumberman fells and removes the merchantable trees, thus opening up the forest floor to the full influence of the sun and wind. The peaty soil quickly dries, fire comes and destroys not only the remaining growing vegetation but also the peat and the organisms in it, thereby rendering the very soil virtually useless for the regrowth of the Taxads and Conifers. When plants of these trees are placed in ordinary garden soil where no humic acid is present, even if there be tubercles on the roots of the plants when brought from the forest, they merely linger and their growth is very slow since the symbiotic organisms are unable to function. This, I believe, briefly is the whole story of the poor regeneration and slow growth of the Taxads and Conifers in the cut-over forests of New Zealand.

CHAPTER XXIX.

Flowers and Ferns

F I could grow one New Zealand flowering tree it should be the lovely *Gaya Lyalli*. This is a large bush or slender branched tree, sometimes 30 feet tall, with Linden-like leaves, more or less persisting through the winter, and clusters of snow-white, inch-broad, saucer-shaped flowers crowding every leaf-axil of the current season's growth; the petals are of a delicate texture, almost translucent, and in the center of each flower nestles a cluster of yellow-anthered stamens. This Gaya and its sister, G. *ribifolia*, brighten at midsummer the alpine scrub and out-skirts of the gloomy Nothofagus forests of the South Island.

The shrubby Speedwells (Veronica) are among the most familiar New Zealand plants in northern gardens. In the northern Hemisphere Speedwells are herbs, often weeds of cultivation, with only here and there a sort of garden value. In New Zealand grow more than 100 species and varieties, some of them large bushes, one (*Veronica gigantea*) a tree 40 feet tall, and many of them very odd in appearance.

One of these (*V. cupressoides*) with scale-like, closely adpressed, bright green leaves looks for all the world like a tiny Cypress; another (*V. lycopodioides*) is like a Club-moss. When in flower their identity is clear but at any other season they puzzle the keenest observer. One of the most common species is the variable *V. salicifolia*, a tall, much-branched shrub with white tinted lilac-color flowers in 6-inch long racemes. An attractive species is *V. Traversii* with racemes of white flowers, another is *V. pinguifolia* with spikes of white blossoms clustered at the ends of the shoots. Loveliest of all is *V. Hulkeana*, a laxly branched, twiggy shrub not more than a yard high, with terminal paniculate clusters of lilac-colored flowers; the panicles are loose, arching and from 6 inches to a foot long and the plant is known by the suggestive name of New Zealand Lilac. It is a very local species found only in the northeastern corner of the South Island. The snowy *V. speciosa* and its forms, with rose to deep blue-purple flowers on stems 1½ feet tall, is one of the handsomest; crossed with *V. salicifolia* and with *V. elliptica*, a species found also in parts of South America, it has given rise to a race of fine hybrids typified by *V. Andersonii* and very much beloved in northern gardens.

On poor soil and where forests have been destroyed a dense thicket of *Leptospermum scoparium* is common over the warmer parts of New Zealand. Known as Manuka, this plant grows from 3 to 10 feet tall and bears white flowers in profusion; occasional bushes are found with double flowers and others with more or less crimson blossoms. A few years ago one of these, named *Nichollsii,* with graceful twiggy stems crowded with rich crimson flowers, created a sensation when exhibited in London. This handsome plant is now well known to Californian gardens.

The Pea-family is one of the largest in the Vegetable Kingdom and its members are prominent in the flora of most parts of the world. Not so in New Zealand, where only thirty-two species belonging to eight genera are known and of these the single genus Carmichaelia claims twenty-one species. These are erect or depressed shrubs, none of which exceed 15 feet in height, frequently of sprawling habit with diffuse, often whip-like, either round or flat branches, green in color, nearly leafless in character, and functioning as leaves. All have small flowers and the plants are more curious than beautiful but are characteristic of physiologically dry regions. Very similar in general appearance of growth and blossom is the related Notospartium with three species, the monotypic Corallospartium and Choniospartium. Another leafless, viciously spiny shrub is *Discaria toumatou,* a member of the Buckthorn family, whose characteristic appearance may be gauged from the name Wild Irishman, commonly applied to this shrub. A curious genus is Corokia, a member of the Dogwood family, of which C. *Cotoneaster* is best known in northern gardens. This is a dense, tortuously branched bush sometimes 8 feet tall with small, often clustered, roundish leaves, gray on the underside, and flowers solitary or from two to four together. There are four species, all of which are evergreen and have yellow flowers. Though widespread in New Zealand they are unknown from any other land.

Among the handsome flowering trees of New Zealand must be counted *Sophora tetraptera* and *S. microphylla,* which grow from 20 to 40 feet tall and by some have been placed in a separate genus called Edwardsia. Both are really small trees with narrow 6-inch long compound leaves, made up of the astonishing number of from twelve to thirty-five pairs of leaflets, and have racemes of large golden yellow peaflowers, each from 1 ½ to 2 inches long. By some botanists these two ornamental trees are regarded as forms of one species and, moreover, are considered to be indigenous also in such widely separated regions as Easter Island, Juan Fernandez and Chile. Another species or variety is *S. prostrata,* a much-branched rigid shrub from 2 to 5 feet high with small bright yellow flowers.

The Fuchsias that make our greenhouses so gay are mainly derived from South American species, especially *F. macrostemma* from Chile, and as showing the relationship with the flora of this continent New Zealand boasts three species of Fuchsia. The best known is the old favorite *F. procumbens* of slender trailing habit and erect petalless flowers which are filled with honey. In these urn-like flowers the pistil is of three lengths and so it is in the flowers of *F. excorticata* which, however, is ofttimes a tree 40 feet tall with trunk clothed with thin, loose papery bark. The third species (*F. Colensoi*) is a shrub with long straggling flexuous branches and flowers in which the pistil is always of uniform length.

Pittosporum with twenty-three species is among the largest group of New Zealand woody plants. These are evergreen shrubs and small trees with handsome often lustrous leaves, and conspicuous, axillary or terminal flowers usually borne in clusters and frequently fragrant. All the twenty-three species are endemic and mostly confined to the North Island. Among the most showy of plants is *Clianthus puniceus*, a much-branched undershrub some 4 to 6 feet tall, with bright scarlet pea-shaped flowers each from 2 to 3 inches long and borne from six to fifteen together in pendulous racemes. It is very rare in a wild state but is much cultivated in New Zealand and well-known in California and Europe. There is also a white-flowered variety but the scarlet type is the more handsome.

Clematis is found wide-spread over the world and in New Zealand nine species are found, all of which are evergreen and have male and female flowers borne on different individuals. The best known and one of the finest of the genus is *C. indivisa*, a stout dioecious climber with lustrous 3-foliolate leaves and axillary clusters of pure white flowers, each from 2 to 4 inches across, the male form being the larger. This Clematis is common, draping bushes and trees and garlanding them in white tresses from August to November. Another species that may be mentioned is *C. afoliata* with axillary clusters of greenish white flowers, and in the adult stage without leaves. This is a very curious plant which forms a dense mass of intertwined stems several feet in length.

A rank-growing climber which in the forest

ascends to the tops of the tallest trees is a Blackberry, *Rubus australis*. The stems, midribs and petioles are armed with stout, sharp, recurved prickles whose tight clinging propensities have won for it the name of Bush-lawyer—when once it takes hold it never lets go! Another remarkable Rubus is *R. cissoides* of scrambling habit which when growing in open, exposed places has the leaves so much reduced that there remain little beyond prickly midribs. There are two other endemic species, one an almost un-armed rambling or climbing shrub (*R. schmidelio-ides*) and the other (*R. parvus*) a little prostrate, creeping thing with one-foliolate bronzy leaves. As if to make amends for the fewness of Blackberry species came the European (*R. fruticosus*) to cover a goodly portion of the land and constitute itself premier pest plant. Cynics declare that there is only one Blackberry bush in all New Zealand, but it stretches itself in an interminable, inpenetrable, inex-tricable thicket throughout the whole length and breadth of the land. A big prize and undying fame awaits the person who devises means of ridding the country of this most unwelcome alien. The Euro-pean Gorse, Sweetbriar, Hawthorn and Watercress are other undesirables which New Zealand would give much to be free of but the Blackberry is the deepest dyed tyrant and usurper of all.

A lofty climber with lustrous green Pandanus-like leaves is *Freycinetia Banksii* which is abundant in the forests, where it climbs and scrambles to the tops of the tallest trees and also makes dense thickets on rocks and fallen tree trunks. The flowers are borne on stout clustered spadices at the ends of the shoots which are enclosed within leafy, fleshy, edible bracts, white or pale-lilac in color, aromatic in flavor and sweet to the palate. In May from among the rich foliage stand oblong, clustered, 6-inch long fleshy red fruits. This is a most striking vine and one which gives much character to the forests.

The most important New Zealand herb from an economic viewpoint is Phormium, which furnishes one of the strongest and most durable of vegetable fibres. There are two species, the best known being *P. tenax* which has leaves from 3 to 9 feet long and dull red flowers on stout stems each from 5 to 15 feet tall and a short erect fruit. The other (*P. Colensoi*) is a smaller plant with yellowish flowers and a pendulous, cylindrical, twisted fruit. Both are found throughout New Zealand; *P. tenax* being the more common in lowland swamps and alluvial soils from sea-level up to 4500 feet altitude. The flowers

of these plants, like those of Clianthus, Dracophyllum, Sophora and the Ratas, are frequented by
honey-sucking birds.

Buttercups are cosmopolitan and rank among the
most familiar of wild flowers and deck with bright
yellow thousands of our northern meadows and
pastures. The species are numerous and their flowers
are showy after a fashion, yet few of our northern
kinds are welcomed in gardens. Most of them are
weeds to be kept without the pale of cultivation.
In New Zealand grow some forty odd species, and
Buttercups form a conspicuous portion of the mountain flora, especially in the South Island. Many of
them possess no more merit in flower and leaf than
our own northern species but others are on an entirely different plane. Indeed, the princes and prin-
cesses and all of the nobility of the whole Buttercup
family flourish in New Zealand. Monarch of all is
Ranunculus Lyallii, a tall, erect plant with leafy,
paniculately branched flowering stems, often 4 feet
tall, bearing as many as thirty snow-white or rarely
cream-colored flowers, each from 2 to 3 inches across.
The basal leaves on long stalks are round or nearly
so, from 6 to 15 inches in diameter, thick in texture
and dark lustrous green. It is so exceedingly common
on the alps of the South Island that in the summer

months the mountain-slopes are white with the abundance of its blossoms. It is known as the Mountain Lily and ranks one of the world's finest alpine flowers. Scarcely less lovely is *R. insignis* with golden yellow flowers, each from 1½ to 2½ inches across, in clusters on stems a yard tall. This is a more or less hairy plant with kidney-shaped leaves 9 inches in diameter. These two species will serve to show the magnificence of New Zealand's Buttercups.

Myosotis, the Forget-me-not genus, much beloved of northern folk, is another group of plants highly developed in New Zealand, where thirty-one species are recognized. Some have flowers of the familiar blue, others have white (*M. albida*), yellow (*M. australis*) or bronze-colored (*M. macrantha*) blossoms. They are an attractive and charming tribe but their beauty wanes before that of their monotypic cousin, the Chatham Island Forget-me-not (*Myosotidium nobile*). This antipodean is a truly noble plant with stout, foot-broad, ovate-cordate or reniform, fleshy dark green leaves, yard-high flower stems terminating in flattened 6-inch broad cymes of dark blue scentless flowers, each one-half inch in diameter. It is a coastal plant, formerly abundant but now owing to the depredations of sheep and pigs is

fast becoming quite rare. Unless granted protection
it will soon disappear and this would bring shame on
the people of New Zealand. Like the magnificent
Buttercups this extraordinary and beautiful plant
has proved well-nigh impossible to cultivate in northern gardens.

The cosmopolitan Daisy family is well to the fore
in New Zealand where a great many of its members
are shrubby and lots of them unusually ornamental.
There are quite a few handsome shrubby Senecios
with yellow flowers but pride of place may well be
given to the Tree-daisy (Olearia) of which there are
many species. All are shrubs from 3 to 20 feet tall
with persistent foliage, in some sorts prickly and
Holly-like, and all bear in quantity flat trusses of
white Daisy-like flower heads. Of the species in cultivation (*O. Haastii, O. macrodonta, O. nummulari-
folia, O. Traversii, O. nitida, O. Hectori* and *O. insignis*) are the best known, but for climates like California all are worthy.

A lovely group of herbs or suffruticose plants is
Celmisia, called Cotton plants on account of the long
white hairs that clothe the leaves. These plants have
Shasta-daisy like heads of flowers, usually solitary
on a foot-long scapes arising from a rosette of oblong
leaves. One of the best and most common is *C. spec-*

tabilis. They are mainly mountain plants and have proved difficult under cultivation. Akin to these are the remarkable Haastias which form large, gray hummock-like masses on barren mountain slopes and whose appearance is well described by their common name Vegetable Sheep. These are among the most singular plants of the whole New Zealand flora.

Speaking of curios one must mention those strange members of the Carrot-family, the Aciphyllas with rigid leaves sharp as bayonets. These are tufted plants of tussock-like habit that strew the higher mountain sides and wage war against all who so much as dare touch them in passing by. One of the most handsome is *A. maxima* with cone-like masses of white flowers terminating stout stalks which rise from amidst the guardian leaves.

An Ice-plant (*Mesembryanthemum australe*) with fleshy pale green or reddish leaves and conspicuous rose-colored or white flowers drapes the coastal cliffs, and in salt-meadows and on rocks close to the sea grows the fleshy stemmed Glasswort (*Salicornia australis*), but these are almost the only true succulents in New Zealand. Only one or two true bulbous plants grow there but she has anomalous plants aplenty of other sorts. Mound or cushion-like,

tufted and tussock-plants are very abundant, especially in the alpine regions and on the stony mountains and dry plains.

A great many plants grow epiphytically in the
forests but the most typical perching plants are the
Astelias belonging to the Lily-family, of which some
ten species are recognized. These form large tufted
clumps on the branches and trunks of trees and also
grow on rocks and even on the ground and are a
prominent feature of the vegetation. They have
panicled masses of small white flowers, the male and
female on different plants, and red, yellow and
purple-black berries.

Orchids are not a conspicuous feature of New Zealand but sixty-five species belonging to twenty-one
genera occur there. Of these six species in four genera
are epiphytes. I may mention the one Dendrobium
(*D. Cunninghamii*), an endemic plant, fairly common from sea-level up to 2000 feet altitude, with
slender, wiry, polished pseudobulbs, each from 1 to
3 feet long, and white and pink blossoms each about
three-fourths of an inch across.

Ferns are universally distributed except in the arid
and ice-clad regions, but being moisture-loving they
are most abundant in the wetter parts of the world.

They reach their greatest exuberance in New Zealand, where in the forests they are a dominant feature and in the open, unforested regions a form of the Common Bracken (*Pteridium aquilinum* var. *esculentum*) is so abundant as to be impenetrable. Forty genera in 140 species grow there but these figures give no adequate idea of the real richness of New Zealand's Fern-flora. The forest floor and every wet rock and tree trunk are crowded with a drapery of rich green Fern and Mosses in abundance. All the familiar tribes are represented except the Royal Fern (Osmunda), yet there is only one endemic genus, namely the monotypic Loxsomia.

Tree-ferns from 6 to 50 feet tall hold one spellbound with their majestic beauty. They crowd the gullies and glens, the forests' edge and depths, and form a green storey that seemingly one could walk upon. Ten different species grow there in millions of individuals. Noblest of all is mighty *Cyathea medullaris*, 50 feet tall with a trunk, 6 feet in girth, oozing black rootlets and armored with the stumps of black stipes; its crown 60 feet broad of twenty to thirty curving dark green fronds, each often 20 feet long and 5 feet broad. The leaf-rachis is covered with glistening black membranous scales among

which are freely mingled prickly tubercles.   In and
around Rotorua I frequently stood awe-struck at the
magnificence of this Black Tree-fern.   Of lesser size
is a sister species, *C. dealbata,* conspicuous on account
of the milk-white under surface of its 40-feet broad
crown of fronds.   Both are well-known in northern
conservatories and so, too, are *Dicksonia fibrosa* and
D. squarrosa of lesser size but equally abundant in
the forests.   The grandeur of the Tree-fern casts a
spell of awe and wonder and man seems a rude in-
truder in their sanctuary.

The Filmy-ferns which gardeners strive so hard
to grow successfully luxuriate in New Zealand, where
the genus Hymenophyllum with twenty species is
the largest group of the entire Fern family.   The
very similar Trichomanes is represented by seven
species.   These charming Ferns, whose delicate pellucid little fronds are ever swathed in moisture,
everywhere clothe rocks and tree trunks in incredible
numbers.

In all the Fern world there is nothing more lovely
than *Todea superba* and *T. pellucida* with stems
from 2 to 3 feet high and 6 to 8 feet broad crowns
of dense plumose fronds, rich green, dripping and
glistening with moisture.   In places these Ferns

crowd the forest flora and in such scenes man's foot-
steps seem profane. New Zealand's Ferns are, indeed, a world of loveliness which to have glimpsed is
sufficient to make a nature-lover's heart throb with
delight and gratitude.